FOREST SCENES

AND

INCIDENTS,

IN

THE WILDS OF NORTH AMERICA;

BEING

A DIARY

OF

A WINTER'S ROUTE

FROM HALIFAX TO THE CANADAS,

AND DURING FOUR MONTHS' RESIDENCE IN THE WOODS ON THE BORDERS OF

LAKES HURON AND SIMCOE.

BY GEORGE HEAD, ESQ.

LONDON:

JOHN MURRAY, ALBEMARLE STREET.

MDCCCXXIX.

COLES CANADIANA COLLECTION

Originally published in 1829
in London, England
by John Murray, Albermarle Street

Facsimile edition reprinted
by COLES PUBLISHING COMPANY, Toronto
© Copyright 1980.

ADVERTISEMENT

TO THE READER.

THAT the journal, the substance of which is contained in the following pages, was never originally intended to meet the public eye, is literally and strictly true.—This fact, in justice to myself, I offer without further comment. And the few years that had intervened since the period to which it immediately relates, had very nearly the effect of suppressing it altogether. But, dwelling with pleasure on the recollections of a country becoming now more interesting every day, and animated by leisure to revise those details written on the spot, which brought the sylvan panorama back to my memory, I found, upon reflection, that there really was much in North America to be described wholly distinct from time or period; perfectly unalterable by change of

scene and lapse of years. And I was further
induced to imagine that, trifling as my own
personal adventures might be, as far as they
related to myself, still, that the sort of life it
was my lot to lead was so unusual, and had
in itself so much of the novel and the curious,
as not to be wholly uninteresting to the plain
reader and the lover of nature. Thus influ-
enced, I have dwelt upon the details of the
forest life; while, on the other hand, I have
glanced over the account of the beaten roads
in a brief and cursory manner; not wishing to
describe what was already sufficiently known,
what has been, and will be again, no doubt,
delineated by abler hands. Still the form of
a diary, which I had adopted, required that
all parts in my journey from Halifax to Lake
Huron (a distance of more than 1200 miles)
should be duly noticed; nor could any, as an
integral part, with reference to the whole, have
been, at all events with propriety, omitted.

If, in this trifling production, I have ever
been induced to venture upon matter not
strictly conformable with its title, it has been

owing to the intimate connection of such matter with my subject, and the irresistible inclination I felt at the moment.   It is now submitted to the world without any pretension.
The anecdotes have been chiefly gleaned in
solitude, and under some disadvantages quite
unnecessary to relate.   But the selection has
been such as will, I trust, present to the reader at least a simple and faithful compilation
of " Forest Scenes and Incidents in the Wilds
of North America."

GEORGE HEAD.

CARSHALTON, SURREY,
   29th MAY, 1829.

CONTENTS.

PAGE

ADVERTISEMENT iii

A few days' residence at Halifax 1

Journey from Halifax to Presque Isle 19

Journey from Presque Isle to Rivière de Cape ... 108

Journey from Rivière de Cape to York, Upper
    Canada 146

Residence in the Woods 178

Summer Journey from Lake Simcoe to Quebec,
    by the Falls of Niagara and the Rapids of the
    St. Lawrence 320

Concluding Remarks on Emigration 351

FOREST SCENES

AND

INCIDENTS,

ETC.

A FEW DAYS' RESIDENCE AT HALIFAX.

IT was in the latter end of the month of November, when I disembarked, after a rough passage from Falmouth, at Halifax, the capital of Nova Scotia, and the passage of the river St. Lawrence being already closed for the winter, it became my duty to undertake a journey over land to the Canadas; I therefore made my arrangements to set out as soon as snow should fall in sufficient quantity to put the roads in good order for travelling in a sleigh. As my stay was not likely to exceed a few days, I went to a sort of hotel and

B

boarding-house, the only description of inn in the place.

The weather, on my arrival, was fine, clear, and generally sunshiny, but accompanied with extremely sharp frost, which had already frozen the ponds in the neighbourhood to a thickness of several inches. Although now on the other side of the Atlantic, I found myself as it were in an English town, among English people, and every thing else much more English in appearance than one would expect to meet with so far distant. But the groups of native Indians were alone sufficient to remind me that I was breathing the air of another hemisphere. These people attracted my earnest attention, for my imagination had painted in high colours the interesting spectacle of man in a state of rugged nature, wild as his native woods, and combining with human intelligence the physical strength of the brute creation. It was not, therefore, without considerable disappointment, that I saw a few squalid miserable-looking beings, straggling in idle listlessness about the streets, and inferior in point of appearance to the wandering race of gipsies in England. One man, with his squaw and a little boy, were by far more tidy and clean than any of the rest. It was on a market-day, and the parents were both sitting down on the ground with things to sell. The man had the skin of an otter and some partridges, and the woman baskets neatly manufactured of birch bark. The little boy was using a bow and blunt arrow very dexterously, by shooting at a halfpenny set up on the top of a stick, which he hit at a distance of twenty yards several times successively. The dress of the man consisted of a close bodied coat of coarse blue cloth, made to lap over in front so as to serve at the same time the purpose of waistcoat and breeches, and from his girdle hung a squirrel skin pouch, in which he carried his tobacco, &c. Instead of shoes, he wore mocassins, made of soft leather, to fit like a stocking, and on his legs pieces of blue cloth, reaching from the knee to the ancle, sewed on tight with an overlap outside the seam, and evidently intended to remain on till they fell off of themselves. His hair, never touched by shears or comb, was as coarse as the mane of a cart-horse, perfectly black, straight, and extremely thick. On such a head, however, he had contrived to stick a coarse felt hat, and, by way of being particularly smart, he had tied round it a piece of scarlet ferret, and part of a dirty shirt made its appearance about his throat. The squaw wore the same sort of mocassins and leggings as her husband, and a short blue cloth petticoat, reaching from the hip to the middle of the leg. Her gown, or rather jacket, hardly reached the petticoat, was carelessly fastened in front, and was made of one of those flaring bed curtain patterns of cotton, full of large red and yellow flowers, birds, pitch-forks, hay-stacks, and cottage scenery. Over her shoulders was thrown a filthy blanket, confined by a skewer instead of a brooch; a bad substitute, for the blanket seemed ready to tumble off. Her long black hair was smoothed straight backwards, and tied, in a club nearly as thick as a man's arm, with a leathern thong. The toilet of both the Indian and his squaw had been completed with abundance of grease of the most rancid description, with which their faces were shining. These two people were in their holiday dress, while others, with scarcely any covering, were to be seen grovelling on the ground, or reeling in a state of intoxication about the streets.

But in Halifax a fair specimen of the North American Indian is not to be met with. Far removed from his natural hunting country, and attracted by the civilized population within narrow peninsular limits, he has sunk into idle debauched habits; and the deleterious effect of cheap rum has destroyed in a very great measure his energies. Notwithstanding these disadvantages, the strength of his constitution is really prodigious. Indians are to be seen at all times in the winter, even under a temperature below zero of Fahrenheit, lying about the streets asleep and drunk, in the open air, with head, hands, feet, and bosom bare; and such is their hardihood, that they are almost proof against being frost bitten. The slow increase of their population, proceeding as it naturally does, without any sort of restraint, is a sufficient testimony of the numbers who perish in the seasoning. Many are the infants, no doubt, who, like blossoms from a tree, fall under the rigours of a few hours' frost; while those who arrive at maturity become fortified by a moral principle which teaches them to consider the endurance of cold and hunger as the extreme of virtue and heroism. The life and habits of the Indian no doubt counteract the increase of his species, for the climate has indisputably a prolific tendency, and there are proofs which might be mentioned, sufficient to establish that fact beyond all contradiction. They are a cowardly race of people, and submit themselves readily to Englishmen, who surpass them in bodily strength as to running, wrestling, and other gymnastic exercises. When they quarrel and fight among themselves, they pull hair and scratch, having no notion of making use of their fists.

Besides their strength of constitution and capability of bearing hunger and fatigue, they possess one faculty altogether wonderful—that of being able to travel point blank across the forest to any given point, let it be an hundred miles off, or farther still; guided solely by an intuition almost supernatural, or by an acuteness of observation such as the human sense would hardly be expected to attain. That a people living continually in the woods should direct their incessant attention to the motions of the heavenly bodies, and profit largely by experience, is no matter of wonder; but we have still to learn how it is that by night, or enveloped in fogs by day, they are able to proceed without the help of sun, star, or compass. It is by the texture of the bark of the trees, rendered coarser on the side opposed to the prevailing winds, that they determine their bearings, although the differences they thus reason upon are so delicate as to be quite imperceptible to an European eye. We know that the acuteness of the senses increases with the intensity of their action, and of this there is no want of instances; those of the shepherd, who learns to distinguish the inexpressive counte-

nances of never so many sheep one from another, the touch of the blind, &c.; but there is
certainly none which has been brought to a
perfection so nearly allied to animal instinct as
the one in question; and the intellectual powers
of the Indians having been wholly unexercised
in any other way, the result is, that such is
their confidence in themselves, that they are
at all times ready to travel alone without the
slightest apprehension, and lie down to rest in
the woods wherever they may happen to be
benighted.

The climate of Halifax does not admit of a
ready comparison with that of England, and
their summer, which lasts about four months,
is not so much hotter as their winter is colder.
They have no season like an English spring,
nor does their autumn resemble ours *.

I had remained very few days at my hotel,

---

* In order to give a better idea, the following Syl-
labus may be useful, to which I should premise that
the weather and temperature in the neighbourhood of
Lake Huron, which will be described in the ensuing
journal, is not far different from that at Halifax, though

when the weather became overcast, with indications of an approaching fall of snow, which,

the range of the thermometer in Quebec is considerably higher in summer and lower in winter.

SYLLABUS OF THE CLIMATE OF HALIFAX, NOVA SCOTIA.

To begin with the months of *July* and *August*. These are the hottest of all, the sun being usually powerful and oppressive. The uniform heat is greater than ours, although a single day in England is now and then nearly as hot as any of theirs.

In *September*, the evenings become cold, with frosts, increasing in severity to the end of the month.

In *October*, the temperature falls perhaps to 25° of Fahrenheit, with rough gales from the north-west, sweeping the frozen continent, and answering to our easterly winds. The weather however is variable, some days still being very warm.

In *November*, a succession of bright sunshiny days generally prevails, and that month is to the Nova Scotian the best in all the year. The fresh frosty air and bright sun have acquired that season the appellation of the Indian summer. The variation of temperature towards the end of the month is very great; sometimes as much as 40° in the twenty-four hours. Some days are close and foggy; others clear and intensely cold.

In *December*, the snow before the middle of the

soon beginning to descend in soft broad flakes,
continued for many hours, till it lay on the

month begins to lie on the ground, the average temperature being about 20°.

January may be called the coldest month ; the average temperature being from 10° to 14°. It drops sometimes 10° or 15° below zero, and remains so for three or
four days together.

February usually commences with extreme cold, the
temperature seldom ranging above 12°. Snow-storms
are violent and frequent. The sun, however, before
the end of the month, shews gradually his increasing
power, and icicles are seen hanging from the roofs of
houses in sheltered situations.

In *March,* clouds of hail and sleet sweep along the
streets with a force hard to be withstood by man or
beast. Cold must be endured in all its variety. On
one day the ground presents to the eye a surface of deep
fresh snow, to wade through which nothing but sheer
necessity would drive a man abroad. Before night
perhaps a fog sets in, with a rapid thaw. Heavy rain
succeeds, and torrents of water and melted snow rush
down the steep streets towards the sea. The compact
mass or cake of ice with which the whole surface of the
ground in the town is covered now begins to make its
appearance, and walking becomes even more disagreeable and dangerous than ever. This mass of ice is full
two feet thick, and it cracks into fissures, which form,

ground to a very considerable depth. The
next morning it had drifted so as to render

as it were, the beds of little rivers, which discharge the
melted snow into the sea.

In *April* the weather is severe and variable. Large
quantities of snow fall during the month, but the heat
of the sun in the middle of the day is too great to allow it to lie long on the ground. Hardly two days are
alike. Sometimes the snow is deep and fresh, at others
soft and sloppy; and again covered with a crackling
coat of ice. Then the north-west wind rages, and calls
forth the powers of the young and active to make way
against its force.

In the month of *May*, the weather has but little improved. The snow falls heavily at intervals, and,
melted by the increased power of the sun, mixes with
mud till the streets are like a bog, and would be considered in any other part of the world impassable. The
variations of temperature are excessive. Keen frosty
winds and a warm sun acting together try the weaker
constitutions. Nevertheless, rheumatic people do not
complain. Those subject to pulmonary attacks suffer
considerably.

In the month of *June* the sun begins to be really
powerful, and in the early part is now and then as hot
as at any time of the year. Yet, the summer has not
arrived, and the trees are only beginning to shew the
first tinge of green. Floating islands of ice, which in-

many parts of the town impassable till a way
had been cleared; and the shopkeepers and
their boys, in fur caps and red nightcaps, with
canvas sleeves over their arms and broad sho-
vels in their hands, were to be seen every
where hard at work throwing aside the snow
accumulated before their dwellings. It had
covered the doors and lower windows of some
of the houses, so that the people were obliged

fest the coast at this season of the year, influence the
climate most considerably. Till these gradually recede,
and, becoming porous, sink to the water's edge, the
weather is never settled and warm. For in the hottest
day, whenever the wind happens to blow from the sea,
it drives before it a dense chilling fog, like a moving
pillar, over the town. There, while it rests, the change
of atmosphere is violent in the extreme. The very
eyes feel wet and cold! And the sea-breeze, which in
England invites the invalid to the coast to inhale its
freshness, drives the Nova Scotian within the walls
of his house. This evil however is of short continu-
ance, for the ice-islands, on whose gelid surfaces these
damp fogs have been engendered, melt by degrees, and,
dispersing themselves over the ocean, cease for the remainder of the year to interfere with the sun's dominion.

to burrow their way like moles into daylight; and one wondered now, at the very beginning of a winter, how the quantities of snow likely to fall during the season could ever be disposed of. The day was particularly fine after the storm; every body seemed busy and animated, and servants were running backwards and forwards with bells, straps, buckles, and harness of all sorts, to prepare for sleigh driving.

At an early hour the first heavy sleighs, laden with wood, coal, and other articles of merchandize, were to be seen laboriously advancing through the deep fresh snow, which becoming by degrees trodden towards the middle of the day, the fresh painted, lighter vehicles were allured from their summer's rest. Then damsels with pretty chins wrapped in fur bade a short adieu to mammas (not here required by custom as chaperones) to take a seat beside their anxious beaux; till smiling faces, tingling bells, and trotting horses were encountered in every corner of the town. Now came the time to look about one: hardly a third part of the space in the street was passable; and as the sleighs came dashing by, one thought oneself lucky, at the expense of a jump up to the hips in a snowbank, to escape being knocked over once in every five minutes. Some of the drivers were good, others bad, but all drove fast, so that, notwithstanding people were obliged by law to have a certain number of bells about their sleigh, the eyes of Argus were insufficient to protect a foot-passenger, who, after all possible pains to get out of the way of the carriages, gained nothing more by way of thanks than snowballs kicked in his face off the heels of the horse. I observed one young man, evidently an inexperienced driver, who was in the act of passing a corner, while he and his fair partner were flying forwards in the original direction long after the horse had completed his turn; and such was the centrifugal motion of the sleigh, that an old woman was knocked down, and the horse completely overcome and brought to the ground by its violence.

Casualties seemed to be perpetually occurring to grave personages, and some of them

sufficiently ridiculous. I saw an old gentleman carefully poking his way across a steep
street with creepers (spikes made to buckle
under the sole) on his feet and a pointed walk-
ing-stick in his hand, when his heels were in
a moment knocked from under him by an ur-
chin in a box placed on iron runners, who shot
down like a flash of lightning from the top of
the hill to the bottom. I picked him up as,
covered with snow, he was puffing with rage
and growling vengeance against the author of
his misfortune. But the old gentleman was
not likely to be gratified; for the boy had
passed like a meteor, and the moment of col-
lision, together with the point of contact, were
the only data by which the sufferer could determine whence he had come and whither he
was gone.

It was quite astonishing to see how the
young people preserved their equilibrium over
parts of the streets covered with ice. The
town consists of long parallel streets, with
others remarkably steep crossing them at right
angles. These latter, in some places where

the snow had drifted away, were covered with a coat of hard ice, over which the young women especially were venturously running and sliding, in groups of three or four at a time, all holding by each other's arms, down such declivities as apparently to put their necks in serious danger.

Waggon loads of frozen pigs were exposed for sale, quite hard and stiff, and in a fit state to keep till the spring. They had an unusually uncouth appearance; for their mouths were generally open, and the last services seemed never to have been properly paid to the defunct. Their limbs were not arranged with decent regularity, and they appeared to have given up the ghost in the act of squalling and at full gallop. Some were placed standing at the doors in the streets, like rocking-horses before a toyshop, upon their four legs, just as if they had been alive. This mode of keeping a pig for a winter without giving him a grain of any thing to eat, or being subject to his noisy, illmannerly conduct,—nay, to be enabled to eat him piecemeal without even the trouble of cutting his throat, is indisputably one advantage of a cold climate. But frozen meat, on the other hand, disappoints the epicure, being always tasteless and bad.

Notwithstanding the day was extremely cold, an auctioneer had established himself at the corner of a street out of doors, and was haranguing a crowd of eager-looking buyers who had assembled about him. Altogether, the appearance of the town after the snow had set in, was, from the novelty of the surrounding objects, particularly lively and interesting to an European.

But while winter brings with it festivities to the inhabitants of Halifax, the sufferings of sea-faring people form a sad reverse. It is indeed an appalling sight to see, in hard weather, a vessel beating up the harbour of Halifax in the teeth of a north-wester. Perhaps from the West Indies! *** On she glides slowly and gloomily through the black waves, her bows and quarters so heavily encrusted with ice, as to be quite disfigured, and weighed down by her head in the water. The sailors,

c

with frost-bitten hands and feet, hanging upon the glassy ropes and rigging, and contending manfully against an unrelenting snow-drift. A few days only have elapsed since the same men, now exposed to the dangers of an iron-bound coast, and a temperature, perhaps, of forty degrees below the freezing point, were broiling under a tropical sun: a change, it would be thought, utterly beyond the power of human nature to withstand.

JOURNEY FROM HALIFAX

TO PRESQUE ISLE.

On the 7th of December a heavy fall of snow which had lasted the two or three preceding days, induced me to make immediate preparation for my journey. I was happy to leave my hotel, kept by a worthy old lady whom I seldom saw. She had prescribed herself a course of the warmer liquors, and had nearly abdicated her authority in favour of the servants of the house, a set of noisy screaming black women. I separated a few necessary articles of equipment from my baggage, the remainder of which I made arrangements to send to Quebec by the first spring vessels. I hired a sleigh to take me and my servant as far as Annapolis, a distance of 132 miles, for which I was to pay twenty pounds, or eighty dollars, including the expenses of the return of the horse and driver to Halifax.

December 8th. At nine o'clock in the

morning my vehicle came to the door. The
snow lay more than a foot on the ground;
besides which, it was still falling heavily. The
wind, also, was full in our faces. I had provided myself, according to the custom of the
place, with snow-boots made of Brussels car-
peting, which buttoned over my boots, reaching above my ancles, with soles of rough felt.
I was further fortified by a good great-coat
and a fur cap with large flaps to cover the
ears. The driver had no sooner got into his
small, seat in front, and urged his horse into a
sort of shuffling walk, than it was quite evident that the animal was at the full extent of
his pace, considering the heavy draft; and we
accordingly travelled at an extremely slow
rate, being full three hours and a half in performing the first fifteen miles.

The soil in the neighbourhood of Halifax is
poor and rocky; and the black granite rocks
and scrubby trees, which shewed their tops
through the snow, looked desolate in the extreme. Land, notwithstanding, in the neighbourhood, sells high; for people, so soon as

they scrape together a little money by farming, flock to the seaports, and reverse the usual order of life by finishing with commerce, instead of retirement. Passing through Sackville, (a small cluster of wooden houses,) we left the extremity of the basin, or arm of the sea, parallel to which the road had hitherto led, and completed a heavy tedious drive of fifteen miles at Mitchell's inn.

The inns in the country are known only by the names of the landlords, to the great discouragement of the profession of sign-painters. The people were not at all uncivil; they allowed me to shake the snow off my clothes in the passage, and proceed unmolested as far as the fire in the parlour; but nobody seemed at all inclined to stir, till, in answer to my repeated entreaties, "Mother," said the great girl of the house, in a fretful tone,—"Mother, don't you hear how the man is calling for something to eat?" and then the mother did begin to move herself, and presently a heavy pile of toast and butter was placed before me, together with tea and beef-steaks. The inn looked like a neat English farm-house. The room was skirted with deal wainscoting, and the furniture was made of the woods of the country. Some articles of birch-wood bore an excellent polish, and those of bird's-eye maple very nearly resembled satin-wood; but the sudden and severe changes of climate had warped them all grievously. A few articles of mahogany also had shared a similar fate. And this evil is universal all over the country, in the best houses as well as the worst. No matter how thick the walls, the tables and chairs always suffer by the weather.

The sides of the room and mantlepiece, were ornamented with trumpery prints of the four quarters of the world in allegory, and plaster of Paris casts of George the Third, Queen Charlotte, and a green parrot with a cherry in his mouth. Every thing looked English, and though a Yankee twang rang in the noses of the country people, giving a marked and provincial accent, yet it was hard to believe one had travelled upwards of two thousand miles to detect so slight a difference

as existed between the people of each side
of the Atlantic.

Two country fellows came into the inn
while I was eating, and placed themselves at
a small table in a corner of the same room.
They called for rum, which was given them
in a vinegar cruet. Glasses were brought,
and then, each passing the back of his hand
across a mighty useful set of teeth, hobbed
and nobbed the other; and, repeating the
ceremony, their little bottle was empty.
Cramming their large paws into their breeches
pockets, the girl of the house was called to a
committee of finance, and, at their request,
replenished the cruet. This second dose made
them sneeze a little, but it was despatched in
as short time as the first. The water now
stood in both their eyes. They had paid for
the rum; hardly a word had been expended
in conversation, and about five minutes of
time had elapsed, when they were out of the
house, and again on their way.

The Nova Scotian peasant, as to his general
appearance, cast of countenance, and accent,

so much resembles the inhabitant of the United
States of America, that a stranger would not
perceive the difference. They have the same
tall, bony, athletic figure; the keen, pene-
trating, inquisitive eye. " They guess and
they calculate", and adopt very many of the
same provincial phrases and expressions. They
are a fine healthy, hardy race of men, in point
of stature certainly exceeding Englishmen.
But the transparent glow of youth is of shorter
duration. Innumerable minute wrinkles (especially about the eyes) appear at a very early
period ; perhaps more owing to the increased
exercise of those particular muscles, which
are brought into a state of contortion by the
sensation of cold; or the dazzling effect of the
sun shining on snow for so many months in
the year, than from any effect produced upon
the constitution. It is, however, very well
known, that the teeth decay particularly soon,
and this, most probably, *is* owing to the cold.
They do not suffer by rheumatism, or any
other disease of that sort. As to clothes, they
take no more precautions than we do. Flan-

nel is even more rarely worn. The man, for instance, who drove my sleigh, sat on his cold perch in front, with no other defence from the weather than an ordinary great coat, such as soldiers wear; without boots upon his legs, or gaiters; merely shoes and worsted stockings.

While the horse was baiting, I took an opportunity of paying a visit to him in the stable; where he was standing in his harness, with the door open behind him, and a rackful of miserably bad hay before him. The building was ill contrived for the purpose of keeping out the wind, had the door been shut; and altogether it was a most comfortless abode for a poor horse. While I was there, the driver came in from the house, and, without rubbing him down, led him out into the yard, and commenced putting to. We went fifteen miles to Rolls's inn, where the horse was baited again; and then proceeded twelve miles more to Burdon's inn, where we put up for the night. It was late when I arrived, and as I was dreadfully cold (for it had snowed the whole of the day) nothing could equal the hospitable appearance of the fire, which was burning in the room. Enormous logs were piled on each other upon the hearth, with a profusion one is quite unaccustomed to in England. Beef steaks were again produced, with tea. I had a clean comfortable bed, and the next morning was ready to start at an early hour.

December 9th.—I proceeded seven miles to Standridge's inn, where I breakfasted. The road was hilly. The day had cleared up, but it had become extremely cold. On both sides of the road, during the whole of the way from Halifax, one could not help remarking the small proportion the cleared land bears to that uncultivated. The trees which, in the neighbourhood of Halifax, are scrubby and stunted, now began to assume a different character, being of much larger growth. Thirteen miles to Graham's inn, Horton township, over a hilly road. Horton was the largest village I had yet seen, small as it was compared to an English one. Having baited, I proceeded fourteen miles to Sharp's inn,

Cornwallis township, over a road tolerably level. Here I put up for the night.

The infancy of the country, as regards cultivation, is most striking; the plough had barely nibbled the edges of the forest, confining itself to the borders of lakes and rivers. And it has been truly enough remarked, that by the proportion which the seams of a coat bear to the cloth ; that which exists between the cleared and wooded surface of the land may be exemplified. Industry seemed to prevail every where, without any apparent vestige of pauperism. The landlords of the inns were usually occupiers of land; and home-made cheeses and cider, both of an excellent quality, were generally produced at table.

December 10th.—Ten miles to Crane's inn, Aylesford township, over a level road. Fifteen miles to Parker's, Wilmot township, over a level road. On this stage I passed the country seat of the Bishop of Nova Scotia; a building of very humble elevation, and not exceeding, in point of appearance, a very

moderate description of English farm-house.
Eight miles and a half to Lennard's, Wilmot
township, over a level road. And here I put
up for the night. The weather had changed
considerably. For more than a couple of
hours, before arriving at the inn, the snow
had become slushy and soft, in consequence of
a very rapid thaw. I had barely got under
cover, when rain began to fall heavily, and
continued till late at night.

The bearing of the people at the inns towards a stranger, is somewhat difficult at first
to understand. They are most of them, as I
have observed, occupiers of land aswell as inn-
keepers; so, not resting a sole reliance on their
inns, they seem to imagine that by admitting a
traveller, they confer a favour on him instead
of themselves; at all events, they treat him as
their equal. In England, it must be confessed,
that civility, however gratifying it may be, is
paid for at a good price. Here, though one
does not get it, it is not charged for in the
bill, and nobody thinks of giving a farthing

to the servants, who, in fact, are most frequently the children of the people of the house.

December 11th.—This morning, on getting into my sleigh, I found the driver beating his hands on his sides, with a short lighted pipe in his mouth. The wind had changed again, and the air was keen and sharp. The frost had set in for some hours, and the roads were improved to a very great degree. Instead of crawling on at the heavy tiresome rate we had hitherto done, a crack of the whip set the horse off at a running trot, which he kept up nearly the whole of the stage, equal to nine miles an hour, as we went over a level road to Spur's, Annapolis township. The road, for the most part, passed through a low level, calculated for feeding cattle, from the abundance of meadow and marsh on both sides. Passed the Annapolis river, which is here about the breadth of the Thames at Staines. We passed it by a bad wooden bridge. Proceeding along its bank, we arrived at the town of Annapolis. The road

was, in many places, exceedingly bad and
rough; for large pieces of rock protruded
themselves above the soil; and against these,
the runners of the sleigh occasionally came in
contact with considerable violence, the snow
not being of sufficient depth to protect them.
The roads, hardened for so great a part of
the year as they are by frost, are less attended
to during the short period of summer. Besides, the soil is rocky, so that a natural road
exists sometimes for many yards together.
Throughout the greatest part of the province,
deficiency of the material cannot be pleaded
in excuse for the bad state of the roads, for
good hard granite is in great plenty. Plaster
of Paris is found in large quantities in the
neighbourhood of Annapolis.

Annapolis, which is one of the largest towns
in the province of Nova Scotia, would hardly
merit the name of a town in England, but
rather of a good sized village; but it may be
observed, that while the natural features of
the country are on a larger scale, the different
grades of society exist on a smaller. Captains

and colonels of militia are to be met with carrying on the trade of publicans, and that not unfrequently ; and the members of the house of assembly, (the colonial parliament,) instead of rolling into their metropolis on easy springs, make their entrée without stile or pretension, jolting in country built buggies*, or, perhaps, bumping side by side on the backs of ambling long-tailed cart horses.

My sleigh was now discharged, having arrived at Annapolis, and I went to Mrs. Crawley's inn, where I was comfortably lodged. I found it by no means an easy matter to procure a vehicle for my journey to Digby, a distance of twenty miles, from which place I was to embark to cross the bay of Fundy to the town of St. John's. I found myself driven to the ne-

* These country gigs possess, nevertheless, nearly the advantage of springs, owing to the body being slung upon pliant poles, spliced on in continuation of the shafts; and the construction is at the same time so extremely simple, that no damage can in probability happen to them, which may not be readily replaced by means of an axe and a few yards of cord.

cessity of making a bargain, an operation not to be effected at Annapolis, without a good many words ; and as every body to whom I applied myself, knew that, as a matter of course, I must go forward, they all hung back, and " tried confusions" accordingly. Some objected to the heavy draft, owing to the soft state of the snow, others had work for their horses on their farms, and so on. At last I came to terms with a man, who said that he would have to send in for his horses, which were several miles from the town; and agreed to give him four pounds to take me the twenty miles to Digby. I had no sooner, however, concluded the bargain, than the cattle were forth coming, never having been out of his stable, and he was as eager to be off as he had appeared before indifferent to the undertaking. Several other proprietors then came and offered me their sleighs at a more reasonable rate ; however, it was too late.

I accepted an invitation to dine with an old gentleman, a Mr. ———. He was more than eighty years old, had served under General Wolfe, and made it a rule to invite to his house all gentlemen in the public service who might happen to pass through the town. He was so perfectly deaf, that it was utterly impossible to converse with him, except by means of a few thirsty interpreters, who drank his port wine, and made themselves otherwise serviceable on social occasions. The old gentleman commenced after dinner to give toasts, after which he called upon his guests in turn for others. Then we were asked to give ladies, and after that, sentiments. And all in such quick succession, that, finding it impossible to do justice to the part I was called on to play, I made as speedy a retreat as I could, and sought the quiet of my inn.

December 12th.—The weather was extremely unsettled, and a thaw had come on in the night, so that when I started, the snow was sloppy, and the roads in consequence very heavy. The sleigh was drawn by two horses working abreast. The way was also hilly; and without an extra horse, it would have been impossible to proceed. In-

deed the thaw had been so rapid, that the
ground in many places was almost bare, and
I occasionally felt the runners of the sleigh
grinding on the bare earth for several yards
together, when it required the utmost power
of the horses to advance. As it was, they
were knocked up before we had gone eighteen
miles. On leaving Annapolis in the morning,
we had proceeded nine miles to Ditman's,
where I breakfasted. This was a small house,
on the banks of Moose river, which is a stream
emptying itself into the Annapolis river. We
then proceeded nine miles to Harris's (making
eighteen miles), where we put up for the night.
We had gone seven miles out of our way, in
order to avoid a horse ford over Bear river.

December 13th.—The frost had set in before the morning, and when the sleigh came
to the door, the air was extremely sharp and
cold. We had a rough hilly drive to the
town of Digby, and a chilling fog added a
blacker hue to the large forest trees on each
side of our narrow route. I was therefore
the more gratified by the sudden appearance

of a splendid sun, setting forth to the greatest advantage a rich sea-view, ornamented by a display of magnificent rock and woodland scenery. The bay of Digby is an outlet of the bay of Fundy, which latter is remarkable for its dangerous navigation, caused by the strong currents and extraordinary swell of its tide, which has been frequently known to rise to a height of sixty feet. Close to the town appears a fine sandy beach, and a regular succession of bluff rocks extend themselves from the head of the bay on both sides towards the sea; and on these, shoals of cormorants, as well as other descriptions of the larger wild fowl, are seen sitting during the day. The bay is circular, and the rocky circumference converging towards the sea, two large corresponding masses of rock overhang each other, forming natural barriers, which leave a narrow passage between, so that vessels enter at once into smooth water. As the road on its approach to the town was circuitous, I had the more leisure to admire the pleasing change of scenery. So few people had occasion to travel on the road I had passed, that solitude and desolation added to the rigors of winter, and the brilliant wood-fires at the inns were the sole comfort and solace of my journey. The long continued exposure to severe cold day after day was a great trial to my patience, though the effects were by no means otherwise injurious. On arriving at the town, I found the only inn full, and was therefore under the necessity of returning three miles on the road I had already travelled, and I put up at a neat little inn, recommended at least by its name, which was " Pleasant Valley." The person who kept the house was a widow, from whom I experienced extreme kindness and attention. Her daughters were well-behaved and exceedingly pretty, and the house was managed altogether with such quiet regularity, that I blessed my stars for the good fortune which had established me in such quarters during the uncertain period of my sojourn in the neighbourhood of Digby.

For the next point in my journey was the town of St. John's, in New Brunswick, towards which I was to cross the bay of Fundy in a small packet which was plying backwards and forwards, and at as regular intervals as the difficult navigation would admit. The distance across is thirty-six miles; but owing to the violent currents, swell of the tide, &c. the passage is never attempted unless with a fair wind and moderate weather. The packet, when I arrived, was not in the harbour, not having returned from its last trip to St. John's; I therefore made arrangements to be informed so soon as she might arrive; and, secure on this point, I made myself quite easy, under all circumstances, at the prospect of being wea-ther-bound under the roof of my kind hostess and her fair daughters. I had the pleasure of seeing what industry and good management could effect in the country; and a house more tidy and scrupulously clean I never entered in any part of the world I ever visited. I went to a large piece of water in the neigbourhood, where I amused myself by skating for a few hours before dinner, which was served in a room warmed by an excellent coal fire, and

furnished with every sort of English comfort.
My landlady was provided with preserved
fruits of every description afforded by the soil,
and these are sufficiently numerous. There
are currants and raspberries, gooseberries,
cranberries, strawberries, apples, pears, and
quinces; and of these she was so liberal, that
I could not satisfy her kind intentions. She
pressed me to eat more of them; " for", said
she, stirring my fire at the same time, " you
will be both cold and hungry before you arrive at Quebec." I thanked her heartily for
her good-will.

I was led involuntarily to think favourably
of a country, in a state of Georgic simplicity;
where a man can build a house in a week;
where, by the help of his gun and fishing im-
plements, there is no chance of his starving;
where, for five shillings an acre, good land
may be purchased, capable of growing wheat,
buckwheat, barley, oats, maize, rye, turnips,
potatoes, &c. I had seen the facility with
which the countrymen wielded the axe, and
had been surprised by the simple mode of

bringing the land first into cultivation. It seemed to me almost incredible, that corn could be grown in a forest of stumps for several succeeding years, merely on the strength of the land, without amendment, except the ashes of the burnt trees; that by merely scratching the surface with a light plough, it could be prepared for the next crop; and that agricultural operations could be carried on with success for a period of ten or twelve years, till the roots of the trees rotted out of the ground of themselves. What if the life of the husbandman be a laborious one? If a man be obliged to work hard for his bread, so long as he has youth and strength, and breathes the air of a bracing climate, why should he not?

The neighbourhood of Digby appeared to me particularly eligible; for the town was a thriving little sea-port: boats of a large size were built in her docks, and the sea abounded with several good sorts of fish. A small species of herring afforded the inhabitants almost a staple commodity. They are extremely delicate, and are salted in great quantities every year. They have gained the nick-name of Digby chickens, and are exported to different parts of the province in barrels.

December 14th and 15th.—The packet not having arrived in the harbour from St. John's, I chiefly amused myself by skating during the day. I also unpacked my gun, and took a walk towards the forest; but the snow lay too deep on the ground for walking without snow-shoes, with which articles I was not as yet provided; neither had I any dog.

December 16th.—I received intelligence that the packet had arrived in the harbour; but upon inquiry learnt that there was no chance of her sailing, unless the wind should happen to change.

December 17th to 21st.—The wind still contrary, and the frost steady and sharp. Both these days I made an attempt to shoot wild-fowl, but without much success. As I was following a large cormorant I had winged, over a salt-water creek which the tide had left dry, I sank into a bog of blue mud, con-

siderably above my knees. In five minutes
the mud was frozen as hard as a stone upon
my clothes, so that I had much difficulty in
walking. Fortunately I was not wetted to
the skin, or I might have suffered from the
accident. As it was, I was obliged to be
thawed when I got home, before I could take
off some of my things. As soon as I had
dressed I went to the house of a man about a
mile distant, to see a dog which had been severely wounded by a species of lynx or wild
cat, which the natives call the loup-cervier, or,
as they pronounce it, the *lousiffee*. The dog
was of the Labrador breed, extremely powerful, and of enormous stature. Notwithstanding his shaggy coat and his ferocity, he very
nearly lost his life in the conflict, by the teeth
and talons of the creature, although the latter
was so inferior in point of size; so much so
as not to exceed perhaps ten pounds weight;
and it made its escape, after a struggle of
three or four minutes, just as the dog's master
had arrived to his assistance. The above description of beast is very scarce.

Wolves and bears are in sufficient numbers through all parts of the forests. As to the former, they are shy and cowardly; for there are enough of deer and other smaller animals to appease their hunger and moderate their ferocity. When they are met with, it is generally singly, or in parcels of two or three together, trotting sluggishly along. But while the wolves lead an independent roaming life, the bears keep nearer to the cultivated land, and in consequence are not on the most neighbourly terms with the farmers. Whenever one is heard of in the neighbourhood, a posse comitatus sally forth with guns and dogs to destroy him. They wage a continual war with the poultry and pigs; and a large bear has been known to enter a farm-yard, seize a heavy fat hog in spite of his remonstrances, and carry his noisy prisoner in his forepaws out of his stye, clambering over rail-fences, and effectually making his escape, notwithstanding the clatter and bustle of men in pursuit of him. Now and then a countryman, armed with a club or a pitchfork, has ventured to bring one to single combat in the woods ; but then he should be, as they call it, " pretty considerable smart," or the bear will whip his weapon with a jerk out of his grasp and come immediately into close quarters, in which case Bruin is pretty sure to floor his opponent. However, they generally run away from a man, and are only at all formidable when they happen to have young to defend.

December 22d. — I was aroused before daylight by the intelligence of the wind having changed ; it was some time, notwithstanding, before the packet heaved anchor, and it was nearly noon before we set sail with a fine breeze out of the bay. The wind was fair, but we were opposed by a violent head current, which caused a short chopping sea. The day was foggy, so that we could but just distinguish Partridge Island as we passed it, which is about a couple of miles from St. John's : a fort and lighthouse are built upon it. In about six hours from the time of leaving Digby, our little sloop (one of thirty-six tons) cast anchor in the harbour of St. John's.

On landing, the difference of climate between the latter place and Digby was very perceptible. In the first place, full half a foot more snow lay on the ground, and the inhabitants themselves estimate a fortnight's difference in the seasons. The town is a good deal smaller than Halifax; and the extreme width of the streets, and the irregular form of the houses, give it a very unfinished appearance. As there was no choice of inns, I went to an hotel of the same description with that in Halifax, and kept by an old widow, who received me with looks as cold as the climate she lived in,—not interesting herself in the least about me, or caring at all whence I had come or whither I was going. It seemed to be with her, as with many others of her description in the country, (if one were to judge by their looks on arriving at their houses,) entirely a matter of caprice whether one was to be admitted or not. She gave me the worst bed-room she had, and dreadfully cold it was.

Different people, at the stated hours of eat-

ing, were in the habit of assembling themselves from various parts of the town. One
or two chewed tobacco; all spit on the car-
pet; and there was one big man who, I was
told, was a lieut.-colonel of the —— militia.
He had a way of eating which I shall never
forget. Closing his teeth upon his knife, he
drew it through his mouth, so as to threaten
its enlargement up to his ear; it was pretty
wide as it was, and as he filled it as full as
it would hold, a sympathetic jerk of his
goggle eyes marked always, by their involun-
tary vibration, the precise moment when each
large morsel passed down his throat. After
tea, a great basin of hot water was brought
to the hostess, in which she washed the tea-
cups and saucers; and then, having deposited
her china in a cupboard, she left me and the
rest of the gentlemen by ourselves for the
evening. The frost set in at night with
great severity, and I found the house miserably cold.

December 23d to 25th. — Sorely against
my will I sojourned these three days at Mrs.

——'s.   Neither entertained nor instructed
by my companions, I was most anxious to get
away at the expense of cold, solitude, or any
other inconvenience.   Fortunately, most of
the party attended only at their meals, and,
having daily business to occupy them in their
shops, (or stores, as they call them,) they
came in with the first dish and disappeared as
soon as the cloth was removed, being obliged,
in fact, to eat against time.   Indeed, they
used admirable despatch, and by blowing into
their soup, and picking bones with their fingers, they contrived to make dinner a very
short business, at the same time devouring
full as much as they paid for.

The next point in my journey was the town
of Fredericton, situated on the river St.
John's, and at a distance of eighty-one miles.
The usual winter route was all the way upon
the ice of the river, but the season was hardly
as yet sufficiently advanced to depend upon
its strength; for however severe the frost may
be, the effect of springs and currents is so
great, that in large sheets of water there are

many particular places most deceitfully unsound, long after the surface generally has
attained a very considerable thickness. Nor
can any period or degree of intensity of frost
suffice to render the travelling upon the rivers
perfectly free from accidents, owing to the
insecurity of the ice ; for the confined air is
continually subject to burst its way from underneath, leaving chasms, which, becoming
immediately lightly skinned over with a new
coat of ice, deceive the traveller by their appearance, and give no warning whatever till
the surface breaks in under the horse's feet :
and these air-holes, as they are called, are
met with at times, no matter what the thickness of the ice may be. The weather was
particularly severe, and seemed to indicate the
established setting in of the winter, and I
agreed with a man for the hire of a two-horse
sleigh from St. John's to Fredericton, and to
set out the next morning. I was to pay seven
pounds on my arrival at the latter place.

December 26th.—It was with much satisfaction that I heard a favourable report of the

state of the river, although it was added, that the passage was frequently exceedingly difficult, owing to the roughness of the ice and the circuitous routes which in many places were indispensably resorted to. I had purchased a buffalo apron, or two skins of the animal sewed together and lined with baize,—an article of the greatest use and comfort: it was to be my friend by day and by night. Of a substance warm as sheepskin and of very large dimensions, my knees and feet were to be defended from the weather during the many hours I must necessarily be exposed to it in open carriages; and it was to supply the insufficiency of covering in the beds and places I should have to lie down in to rest at night. My sleigh came to the door early in the morning; and when I left St. John's the thermometer stood at 12° of Fahrenheit. The driver occupied a small seat in front, and was a rough-looking fellow both in dress and countenance. He wore a huge cap made of the skin of a fox, and the brush was sewed across the top of it fore and aft, like the cone of a

helmet. A black stump of a tobacco-pipe
was in his mouth. He had a close-bodied
coat on his back, made of a blanket, with a
sash of red worsted round his waist. Cracking his short whip, he urged the horses
through the streets at their best speed,
which it soon became necessary to slacken;
for the first stage was remarkably rough and
hilly. We proceeded very slowly till we arrived at an inn, called Poverty-hall, where
we baited.

We had now arrived on the banks of a small
river which empties itself into the river St.
John's. As soon as the horses were ready to
start, I got into the sleigh tolerably refreshed,
and the broad scorched face and replenished
pipe of the driver were sufficient, had I any
fears on his account, to entirely dissipate
them. The perspiration of the horses had
frozen upon them, but they looked healthy
notwithstanding. We now prepared for a
drive on the river; and at first making our
way slowly over fragments of broken ice and
congelated heaps of snow, we came at last to

E

a sudden dip, and then were carried away forwards with a launch upon the bed of the river. The wind had cleared away the snow, and the ice was nearly bare. The driver rattled his horses on at a brisk gallop, till they by degrees settled down into their fastest trot. The sound of the runners upon the ice and of the horses' feet, together with the perfect indifference with which the driver treated repeated loud cracks, which were distinctly audible, was to me altogether new. Still the motion was agreeable, and the labour of the horses so light, that there was very much to be pleased with; so, finding that he whose business it was to judge of the soundness of the ice was satisfied, I very soon left off thinking about it.

We proceeded this stage of eleven miles to Gidney's all the way on the river, which is in most places about three quarters of a mile broad. Thence ten miles more to Wurdon's: five miles of this road, through the forest, were particularly rough and bad. We then began to descend, and reached the ice again at

Lyon's Creek, which is an arm of Belleisle
Bay. We passed along the creek, and the
wide expanding shores of the bay appeared in
front of us : it is about twelve miles long and
three broad, and, owing to the sweeping gusts
of wind which had incessantly passed over its
surface, it presented to the eye an uniform
sheet of clear ice; and here we were roused
to life and animation by a brisk and long-
continued gallop, both the horses laying their
ears back and biting at each other all the
time. After the dull, heavy drag of the first
part of the stage through the wood, the
change of pace and of scene altogether was
in a great degree enlivening; the quick jingle
of the bells and the excitement of the horses
added a deeper hue to the purple cheeks of
the driver, who sat on his seat singing, while,
with his whip under his arm, he was striking
fire for a fresh pipe ; — and thus we spun
along till we came to Wurdon's. And now
we had arrived upon the St. John's river,
whose course I was to follow for nearly 300
miles.

A dreary and a rugged desolation had hitherto marked the features of the path I had travelled,— a heavy uninteresting sameness everywhere pervaded the landscape; but now the scene was varied by bays and creeks, and hour after hour the wide difference in climate and general appearance between North America and England became more and more striking. Certainly, there are no two countries more thoroughly different. An interminable extent of forest land, covered with snow during a long and rigorous winter, presents in itself a gloomy view of inanimate life; a melancholy stillness, totally unlike the cultivated face of nature under a more genial climate. It is true, that the slow but increasing process of agriculture may work important change; the axe may level the forest with the earth, and the cheering beams of the sun, admitted to its hidden recesses, may dissipate the masses of snow which now feed the piercing winds of winter: but the greater the extent of land laid bare, the greater contrast must necessarily shew itself; as rivers, lakes,

rapids, and waterfalls everywhere becoming
developed, demonstrate an increased scale of
grandeur truly worthy of admiration.

We travelled eight miles farther to Gold-
ing's, the track being the whole of the way
on the river. The cold was very intense, and
a covering of six inches of snow lay on the ice.
The average breadth of the river, subject here
to considerable swells and torrents, was about
half a mile ; but it became often much wider,
and a degree of wildness and irregularity
added interest to the appearance of the country as I proceeded on my journey.

December 27th.—The weather this morning continued extremely cold ; but we started early, and proceeded along the ice on the
bed of the river fourteen miles to Dale's.
We saved three miles by leaving the river on
our right and pursuing our course overland.
The tide is here remarkably rapid, and there
are a number of lakes in the neighbourhood :
of these, the Grand Lake is thirty miles long
and nine broad, and is distant about three
miles.

Having baited, we proceeded nearly four miles up the river, when the ice exhibited an appearance not very encouraging. Large serpentine tracks of water were to be seen in many parts, and heaps of broken ice, forced up by the strength of the current, lay ranged on each side in considerable profusion. From some country people whom we met we were told, that the passage was not safe; but that the road on the opposite bank was already sufficiently broken to render it tolerably good. The driver, therefore, bore away for the shore, which we were some time in reaching, being obliged to go out of our way frequently to avoid the weak and unsafe places. At last, when within about a couple of hundred yards from the land, there seemed a clear sheet of ice, over which the driver urged his horses at a brisk trot; when all at once the ice suddenly gave way, and down went the horses head foremost into a hole. We were going so fast, that I was flung out a long way clear of the water; and as soon as I could get up, I ran back to render my assistance. One of

the horses had already scrambled out, but
the other was lying on his side in the water,
with his head stretched out over the forward end of the hole, and supporting himself by his cheek and all the strength of his
neck on the ice. The hole was nearly round,
and the diameter rather more than the length
of the horse; but as the ice about it was full a
foot and a half thick, the sleigh had jammed
at the other end, and his hind quarters were
supported by the breeching. The poor creature lay without struggling, although the
day was bitter cold, and he had sunk so low,
that his head only was above the surface of
the water. In this dilemma the driver, having freed the other horse from his harness,
slipped a noose of rope round the drowning
animal's neck, upon which we pulled till he
seemed nearly strangled : and this operation
is called in the country, very properly,
" choking." Whether it was that he floated
by means of the air thus forcibly retained in
his lungs, as the driver asserted, or whether
our united efforts caused him to rise, I cannot

say; but so he did: and we had not continued
to tug long, before out he slipped on his side,
and, after a few kicks and struggles, stood
frightened and shivering once more on his feet
on the ice. We got to the shore after all
with some difficulty; for the ice was broken
away for so great a distance from the edge of
the river where we attempted to land, that it
was with very great labour that the horses
could drag the vehicle over the hard snow and
shingle which obstructed their progress. Although the poor horse had been nearly a quarter
of an hour in the water, and the other also was
perfectly wet from the accident, both soon recovered themselves, and before we had gone a
couple of miles were quite as well as ever.

The above may be cited as an instance of
the hardihood of the North American horse,
of which less care is taken, notwithstanding
the severity of the climate, than in England.
The cold, severe as it is, seems to agree with
them very well, and they are continually kept
standing out of doors, without mercy, after
being violently heated. The fact is, that the

cold keeps down all tendency to inflammatory attacks, and a striking instance of this occurs with regard to flesh wounds. They are frequently receiving injuries between hair and hoof from the calk or spike of the frosted shoe, so severe as would be reckoned a serious accident in England; however, they are worked invariably without bad consequences, and few of the farmers' horses are to be met with whose hoofs do not shew a succession of scars, which remain till pared away in process of time, at the bottom, by the blacksmith. Many of the horses of the country have good blood, being the progeny of stock formerly imported by the Duke of Kent; and others of good substance and action are now and then brought from the United States. The hay is bad everywhere,—like Irish hay, dried without being allowed to heat, and then thrown into a barn or stacked under an open shed. Notwithstanding all these disadvantages, to which it may be added, that the stables generally are miserably protected from the weather, horses now and then arrive from England, very soon

become perfectly reconciled to all their difficulties, and thrive as well as the rest.

We travelled very slowly, slipping and jolting for about six miles parallel to the river.
We were obliged to cross over two very bad
wooden bridges, formed of loose logs laid
close together, which the horses' feet at every
step threatened to displace. These streams
formed a communication between the river
and lake Macquancup, which lake is about
five miles long and three broad. The distance
of this stage from Dale's to Tilley's is nine
miles. Major's Island, situated opposite the
latter house, is about three miles long and one
broad, and the property of a man who, with
three of his tenants, lives upon it. A few hundred acres only are cleared.

Having baited at Tilley's, we proceeded
ten miles more to Pelley's, the road all the
way being on the bank of the river. It became, however, better and better as we approached the town of Fredericton, and we met
many more people on the road than usual.
Although it was quite dark when we arrived

at Pelley's, the driver was inclined to proceed ten miles more to Fredericton, the road to which place lay all the way on the bank of the river. We did not come upon the ice till we had arrived nearly opposite the town,— not from the apprehension of its being unsafe, but from the quantity of snow which lay upon it, (it was more than a foot deep,) and would have added so much to the labour of the horses. No snow had fallen, as we were informed, during the period we had been on our way from St. John's, notwithstanding it lay so much deeper on the ground here than at the latter place. I had suffered dreadfully from the cold during this day's journey; and as the people at the inn were in bed and the fires low when we arrived, nothing remained but to ask permission to go to bed too. A sleepy black woman ushered me into a comfortless apartment, where the bedclothes and my own buffalo skin together were quite insufficient to restore warmth. Every five minutes I lamented my want of covering, while a powerful inclination to sleep urged

me to patience in the forlorn hope of rest.
The thermometer was about 10° of Fahrenheit.

December 28th.—Daylight no sooner appeared than I eagerly sought relief; and
dressing myself as quickly as my benumbed
fingers would allow, I went down stairs to
the apartment below, where the fire was just
beginning to blaze. I had suffered not only
from cold during the night, but from hunger;
but now all my miseries were dissipated with
the smoke which went up the chimney, and a
solid meat breakfast put me completely to
rights. Afterwards I took a rapid walk, and
on returning to the inn found a card lying on
my table from the managers of a subscription
assembly, which was to be held the same
evening in the town. As a few days' halt
for the purposes of equipment for my journey
was indispensable, I did not hesitate to ac-
cept the invitation, and took measures to hire
a sleigh to take me to the assembly-room,
about a mile from the inn.

Soon after I had dined at an early hour, I
got into the sleigh, and in a very few minutes

was conveyed at a rapid pace to the assembly-room, which I found remarkably well lighted, and garnished with ladies, both old and young, with the usual proportion of card-players, &c. Most of the gentlemen wore boots with heavy iron heels, the noise of which, as they paraded the room in threes and fours between the dances, produced a prodigious effect, and created a wonderfully military appearance. As to the young ladies, they were, as in most parts of the world under similar circumstances, all in their best looks and extremely engaging; but the time of all others when they made the most impression was at a late hour in the evening, at the general rush into the cloak and bonnet rooms.

Hitherto matters had been conducted without any very striking difference from similar festivities at home ; but now the jingling of the bells of the sleighs outside the door, and the preparations of the ladies within, began to savour of novelty. All wore snow boots, or list coverings for their feet and ancles, which were buttoned, or laced, or tied, something after the manner of a half-boot; and heaps of these were distributed, by the person who had them in charge, to their fair owners; who all at once, within a very small space, began to put them on.   All these snow boots required fastening, and to fasten them it was indispensable to stoop : some had chairs, but most had not; so that the variety of attitudes in which the female figure was on that occasion displayed, I shall not readily forget,—much less the dilemma in which I found myself when, standing in the midst, and surrounded by so many fine forms, I was unable to stir an inch to the right or left, backwards or forwards, without the imminent risk of disturbing their equilibrium.   But they equipped themselves with great rapidity; and laden with shawls, plaids, and calashes, sleigh after sleigh received its burden, and away they went with bells jingling and the white smoke from the horses' nostrils shining in the lamps of the remaining carriages.

December 29th.—I employed myself this day in procuring several necessary articles for my ensuing journey. I had now eighty-three miles to Presque Isle, which was the ultimate point passable by any sort of carriage; the usual route from thence to the St. Lawrence being along the bed of the river St. John's, which is so wide and exposed to the force of the wind, that the depth of the snow is by far too great to pass in any other way than on foot by the help of snow shoes. The traffic, too, is very inconsiderable, as the fatigue of such a mode of travelling deters people from attempting it; and the communication is kept open by a line of small log-houses, occupied by settlers, to whom grants of land have been ceded for the especial purpose. There is a very small military station at Presque Isle: and across the desolate track above mentioned, extending for upwards of 150 miles, the post is conveyed by native Canadians, who are from time to time accompanied by those persons whom urgent business may, though rarely, induce to undertake the journey.

It was for this route that it was now necessary to equip; for after leaving Fredericton there was no town nor village at which the required articles could be procured : namely, a couple of tobogins, a tobogin bag, a canteen, havresac, some pairs of mocassins, two pairs of snow shoes for myself and servant, together with other trifling things. A tobogin is a small sleigh, drawn by men, of very simple construction, and capable of conveying from 100 to 140 pounds of clothes or other baggage. It is made of quarter-inch plank, about a foot and a half broad and eight feet long; the forward end is bent upwards, so as the more readily to pass over any obstructing body. A set of small holes are bored on each side; and the tobogin bag when full is then laced tightly on the machine by means of a cord. The whole thus forms a compact mass, so secure that it may be tumbled and tossed, dragged among stumps of trees, and rolled over and over in the snow, and after all be not a whit the worse at the journey's end. Dogs also are frequently used to draw them.

As to the mocassins, the common ones, generally worn by the country people, are made of ox hide; and those of a better description, of the skin of the deer. The hide of the moose deer furnishes the very best, but they are scarce; as the animal, equal in size to the Russian elk, is of a race nearly extinct; a few only are killed every year in the spring, when there is a glassy surface or crust over the snow hard enough to bear the hunters on their snow shoes, while it breaks in under the heavy creature, which is thus easily tracked by his foot-marks. The mocassins intended for travelling are of a much larger size than the common ones; for, besides other coverings, the foot is wrapped in a piece of blanket cut for the purpose, about fourteen inches long and eight wide, and then thrust into the mocassin, which is secured firmly by long thongs of soft leather passing round the ancles. As the upper part of the mocassin is composed of loose flaps, by this method the foot has an excellent protection, and is kept warm and fit for the day's journey, either with or without snow shoes.

A moderate sized snow shoe, being a light

wooden frame of an oval shape, is about forty inches long, and eighteen in extreme breadth, and its weight is about two pounds. The whole surface within is formed of a net-work of thong, like that of a racket, but rather stouter. A small square aperture, about the size of a man's hand, is left in the net-work, into which the toes sink at every step, by which means the foot is prevented from slipping back, and a purchase is given to step from, while the snow shoe, forming an artificial platform, remains still on the ground. The foot is in no way confined to the machine, except by the toes, by which it is lifted, or rather dragged along at each step. Although less previous practice than one would at first imagine is necessary to walk on snow shoes, still a novice commences a journey under very considerable disadvantage. Indeed, so certain is the effect produced by the exercise upon persons not trained to it, that the Canadians have a name for the complaint it brings on. They call it the " *mal à raquette*", which is a violent inflammation and swelling of the instep and ancles, attended

with severe pain and lameness. A journey on
snow shoes cannot, at all events, be undertaken
under greater disadvantages than by a person newly arrived in a strange country and
climate, fresh from a sea voyage. Much is
said by the natives of the superiority of such
a mode of travelling over any other; but, in
spite of all their wonderful stories, a very
little practice will put an end to the pleasing
anticipation of a journey on snow shoes (unless a very short one) by way of amusement;
and I never saw any body who, after a reasonable trial, was not most heartily glad to
kick them off his feet, and at the same time
to make up his mind to walk during the remaining days of his life without their assistance.

There was a large Canada stove in the
kitchen of the inn, or hotel, where I had
taken up my abode, which was, during the
day, a favourite resort for the country people
and other customers of the house; and a talk-
ative noisy set was constantly kept up by the
comers in and goers out. Among the most
regular in attendance was an old Indian, who,

leaving his squaw to take care of the wigwam, which was in the neighbourhood, made
this kitchen his morning lounge—his club as it
were, where he heard the news, saw how the
world was going on, and drank as much rum
as the different visitors were inclined to give
him. To this man I introduced myself, and,
as he spoke English, and understood it very
tolerably, I made an appointment with him
the next morning. He agreed to come to me
at the inn, where I was to treat him with
plenty of rum, so as to make him feel quite
comfortable, and then we were to take a walk
together, he on his snow shoes, and I on mine,
as far as the wigwams, a few miles out of the
town, where I was to have the honour of
being presented to his squaw and family.
Novelties, therefore, after much cold, stupid
travelling, appeared at last to be on the point
of arriving.

December 30th.—The old Indian was true
to his appointment, and before nine o'clock
I had scarcely finished my breakfast, when he
walked into my room, saying, " May be mas-

ter has got a little rum." Thinking that whiskey probably would do as well I filled a large wine glass which was upon the sideboard, and he drank it without coughing or sneezing. Eternal friendship beamed from his small deep-set black eyes. The fire was beginning rapidly to extract the odours of his toilette, and he drew himself closer and closer towards me, while he commenced a narration relating particularly to his own address and bravery during the late American war. The glass of spirits had not been evidently the first which he had swallowed that morning, for his story was frequently delayed by the slaver which flowed from his mouth, and the indolent paralysis of his tongue. A buck-shot which he had received from the enemy, and which remained in his thigh, was the leading topic of his conversation, and as his language became more and more indistinct, his gesticulations were proportionably violent as he described his manner of crouching, advancing, and firing upon the foe. I endeavoured to quiet him, and remind him of the purpose of his visit, by shewing him my snow shoes and patting him on the shoulder with heavy thumps, in order to bring him to his recollection. But his subject interested him so warmly, that he would not listen to reason. He raved about his scars and his cuts, and " Look ye ", said he, " Indian man shew master the buck-shot." At the same time drawing aside the flap of his close bodied coat of coarse blue cloth, he exhibited a thigh so tough and stringy, as might, one would have thought, have been quite shot proof; notwithstanding there lay the object of his boasting, quite visible under the skin. The exhibition was the more simple, inasmuch as he wore no breeches.

At last I got rid of him, when, very fortunately for me, he encountered the landlady, to whom, in the presence of the little world of the inn, he insisted upon shewing, *à-propos* to nothing, the buck-shot. This so enraged her, that with a *posse comitatus* of her maids, black and white, they, by the help of brooms and mops, turned him forthwith out of doors into the street. And now, by the help of some men who were outside, we at last induced him to make a virtue of necessity. So, finding that the doors of the house were shut against him, that he could get no more rum from any body on the spot, and having obtained a promise from me of a liberal quantity so soon as ever he should have acquitted himself of his undertaking, he began with great gravity and silence to tie on his snow shoes, and, lighting a short black stump of a tobacco pipe, which he took out of his pouch, he commenced walking away with long strides, without looking behind him, and leaving me to follow as well as I could. My snow shoes had been on some time, while I waited with impatience the drunken dilatory loitering of this savage: but now the pace he was going, obliged me to exert myself to the utmost to keep up to him. Puffing and smoking, he walked on, and his gaunt sinewy frame was continually gaining ground on me, when the point of my snow shoe catching in the snow, tripped me up. As I found it in vain to rise immediately, from the manner in which my feet were hampered, I was obliged to call out to my guide. He returned to my assistance, but, with very great difficulty, I had contrived to get upon my legs before he came up. And this accident occurred three or four times in the first mile, after which I began to acquire the little practice necessary to keep upon my feet. Still I found the labour so much greater than I had imagined, that I was almost inclined to wish I had remained at Halifax till the spring, to have proceeded then by the St. Lawrence to Quebec. But now it was too late; here I was, and on I must go, *coute qui coute.* We had left the road at the outskirts of the town, and had proceeded in a straight line for nearly three miles, when some smoke, which appeared rising at a little distance, marked the situation of the wigwams we had come to see. There were twenty or thirty of them; and I soon found myself arrived at the *dulce domum* of my old guide.

A wigwam is like a bundle of hop-poles, as they are piled in England during the summer; that is, it is shaped like a cone, and a

little larger than an ordinary tent. It is
formed of long poles, the ends of which are
placed on the ground in the circumference of
a circle, the points being brought together
and confined at the top. It is thatched from
the bottom to within a couple of feet of the
top, with the boughs of the spruce fir, and
large strips of birch bark; so that, in order for
the smoke to escape, an aperture is left at the
top, through which no snow enters, from the
current of air passing upwards. Rain is not
calculated upon in the winter. The wigwam
within side, rude as it is fashioned, is exceedingly warm, and not particularly incommoded
with smoke; for, from its figure, the greater
quantity of air being at the bottom, and becoming heated by the fire, a current is created
of sufficient force to oppose the smaller quantity towards the top. The fire is made in the
middle, and the whole family sleep with their
feet towards it.

The old Indian had been rather out of humour and sulky; for he had not forgiven the
treatment he had received from the landlady

of the inn; but now arrived at his own fire-
side, his heart began to warm again, and I
saw, by his gestures, that he was relating to
his squaw his own troubles and our adventures during our walk from the inn. The
squaw seemed to be many years younger of
the two, and she was sitting on the ground
busily at work, ornamenting a pair of mocassins with coloured porcupine quills. Her mother, a very old woman, was swinging a child
bound up, like an Egyptian mummy, in swad-
dling clothes, strapped down fast and tight on
a board, and suspended on a peg from the
upper part of the wigwam. Whenever the
child cried, a touch on the board with her
hand set it swinging, so as to answer fully the
purposes of a cradle. A boy of about ten
years old was making a wooden spoon out of
a piece of maple, which he hollowed for his
purpose with a large, broad, square pointed
knife. There were also a little dog and a cat,
both of a lean and starved appearance. As
to furniture, there was none, except a rusty
gun, a rum bottle, and a tin saucepan. The

family sat upon logs of wood, and slept in
their clothes, such as they were. Although
the day was exceedingly cold, the inside of this
hut was warmer than the room of any house.
My guide took me into some of the other
wigwams, where we found very few men at
home. The women were invariably employed
very busily, some working at their needle,
others making brooms, small baskets of birch
bark, and other trifles of the same sort. I
was, however, very soon satisfied with what I
saw, and prepared to return to my inn, being
happy to leave the dirty wigwams, glad of
the opportunity of walking more leisurely
home, and not at all sorry to get rid of a
drunken companion.

There is nothing, perhaps, which proves the
resources of the country more than the dissipated and improvident habits of the native
Indian. With no other dependence than a ten
shilling Birmingham gun, a little coarse gun-
powder, and some Bristol shot; his fishing im-
plements, and a coarse home-made bow and
arrows; he relies upon chance each day for his

food.   If successful, he gorges; sometimes he
fasts; to-morrow never enters into his head;
and whenever, and as often as he possibly can,
he gets thoroughly drunk.   In spite of all this,
the forests and rivers supply him continually
with food, and in sufficient profusion; and a
rooted antipathy to every sort of labour, together with his wandering habits, have hitherto
set at defiance all efforts to reclaim his race.
If, therefore, the idle and improvident find
the means to provide themselves against the
wants of nature, surely the hard-working and
industrious have even a better prospect of success.

I walked back to my inn, but not without
difficulty.   I found my way by the foot-marks
which remained on the snow, but I felt disappointed at the result of my first day's practice
on snow shoes.

December 31st.—Having now every thing
ready, I had to make the best of my way to
Presque Isle, so as to arrive there about the
time of the postmen, on their way to Quebec.
I preferred accompanying these men to hiring

an Indian as a guide, and had at first determined to wait at Fredericton till they arrived
in the town from St. John's. Growing impatient however, I determined to start the
next morning, and at all events to leave Fredericton, and get to Presque Isle as quick as
I could. I accordingly engaged a two horse
sleigh from a French inhabitant, who agreed
to take me the eighty-three miles, and return
with his horse and sleigh at his own expense
to Fredericton for eight guineas.

January 1st.—It was nearly noon when the
man made his appearance with his sleigh, a
tardiness which but ill accorded with the state
of the roads. With the river on our right,
we proceeded along its bank through snow so
deep and untrodden, that with the greatest
labour and difficulty we advanced, literally
speaking, at a ploughing pace. We reached
the house of the owner of the sleigh, where
we baited. We then proceeded on our journey, and crawled on six miles more, and put
up for the night at Upper French Village. It
was near seven o'clock when we arrived and

we had been nearly all the time since noon going sixteen miles.

The house we were now in for the night was very particularly dirty and comfortless. There were two beds in the room, one for the host, his wife, and four children, (the youngest of which was not more than a few weeks old,) and the other was appropriated to me. The driver and my servant lay on the boards before the stove, which was a Canada one, and too powerful for the size of the room. The heat all night was quite suffocating, though the weather certainly was not warmer than 20° of Fahrenheit. The bed I slept in had green stuff curtains, full of dust; and the sheets were of some soft spongy material which, if clean, at least felt otherwise, and for the first time since I had been in the country, I was tormented with fleas. It was impossible to get a wink of sleep; for, besides my own grievances, there were other causes of disturbance. The child cried incessantly in spite of all the woman could do to pacify it. It had, I believe, nothing at all the matter with it, but seemed,

from sheer frowardness, to imagine that the
little world of our miserable apartment was
made for itself. Sometimes the good wife sat
up in her bed with the little animal hugged
up between her chin and her elbows, hushing
and rocking herself and it; then she patted
its back, and still it cried. Then ten times (I
dare say) in the course of the night, out of
bed got the poor husband, and stood for several minutes at the stove, with a pair of lean
bare legs, and an extremely short shirt, stirring something in a saucepan with the broken
stump of an iron spoon. A picture of obedi-
ence and misery! Then he got into bed again.
Then came a long consultation, and almost
a quarrel, about what was best to be done.
Then the grand specific was administered,
but all without effect. At last the other
children awoke, and the youngest of these
began to cry too: and the mother said it was
the big one's fault, and beat her. So off she
went, and we had a loud concert, till, what
with the noise of the children, and the heat,
and the dirt, and the fleas, I felt ready to rush

out of doors and roll myself in the snow. But every thing must have an end, and so at last the children became all tired out, and by degrees grew quiet; and in the morning I found I had been asleep, and got out of bed determined to be off as soon as I possibly could.

January 2d.—It was before sun-rise when the sleigh came to the door, and I got into it, happy to exchange the fusty exhalations of this room, for the piercing cold of a Canadian winter's morning. We proceeded ten miles to Ingram's, by a road equally bad with the one we had travelled the day before. The snow was just as deep, and the way not more broken; therefore our pace was still a slow walk, occasionally delayed by drifts, through which the cattle could only make their way by courage and floundering on with all their might. Sometimes they stopped short, and with distended nostrils, and eyes expressive of fear, they seemed inclined to give it up altogether. But they were both high-spirited animals, and we were indebted to them for overcoming difficulties, which a person less experienced than the driver would have hesitated to set their faces to.

Occasionally, during this stage, we encountered some little ravines, or precipitous gullies, which crossed the road, and which formed small creeks or outlets of the river. There were several of these which it was necessary to pass, and at the bottom of each was a rude wooden bridge without side-rails, and scarcely broad enough to permit three horses to pass abreast; notwithstanding which, we went over with our pair always at full gallop: much to my annoyance at first, till I found that the cattle possessed quite as much sense as their driver, and sufficiently understood what they were about. The ravines were so steep, that in order to ascend one side, it was absolutely necessary to rush down the other to gain an impetus; and the distance from the top to the bottom was about 150 yards. The bridges were composed of pine logs laid loosely together, which made a rattling and a clatter as the horses' feet came upon them. The French-

G

man drove with long cord reins, without any contrivance to prevent them falling down the horses' sides, and the rest of the tackling was of an equally simple fashion. The cattle were indeed but barely attached to the vehicle; a matter of little importance during the former part of the journey, but now deserving a little more consideration: for the horses, so sure as they arrived at the verge of each ravine, seemed to take all sort of charge upon themselves, while the driver, yielding to circumstances, sat still upon his seat. Up went their heads and tails, and, like a pair of hippogrifs, down they went with a dash till they reached the bridge, when, closing together, laying back their ears, and cringing in their backs, they rattled over the logs at full gallop, and up the opposite bank, till the weight of the vehicle brought them to a walk. Now came the turn of the driver; and as he was perfect in all the words which frighten horses, he used them with such emphasis, jumping out of the sleigh at the same time with considerable activity, while the animals dragged it through the deep snow, that he contrived to keep them to their collar till they had completed the ascent.

Some address was required to prevent being thrown out of the vehicle by the violence of the motion. It was absolutely necessary to retain fast hold of the side; and then the thumps and jerks were such as cannot be readily imagined. Nothing, in fact, can be worse than the motion of a sleigh on a rough road. There is a grinding sensation which threatens the breaking up of the whole machine. It feels as if parting in the middle and going asunder. The jolts inflicted by lumps of hard snow and other obstacles, may be compared to the blows of a short chopping sea upon a boat making head-way against wind and tide. The bones rattle by the concussion, as one helplessly submits to discipline as rigid as an unfortunate infant, when violently shaken by a passionate and drunken nurse. Our sleigh was dragged heavily along, while the horses frequently came to a stand still.

The whole of the distance of this stage, the

G 2

forest abounded with shumac and hemlock trees; the former well known as an ornamental shrub in England, and the latter a stately species of fir growing to a large size, with a remarkably small leaf, and the wood particularly adapted to purposes which require it to remain under water. The greater part of the way from Fredericton, the ice would very probably have been sufficiently firm to have borne our sleigh, but we were advancing into inhospitable regions, where the traffic becoming less and less, the road had been but little beaten, and the bed of the river had not been used at all. Houses were now so scarce that the country seemed altogether deserted; not a bird was to be seen, except now and then a solitary wood-pecker: the only species left to its winter habitation. Had a fall of snow increased our difficulties, recourse must have been had to our snow shoes. The horses were in a continual foam from dead pulls, and floundering out of holes formed under the snow by the roots of trees which had rotted out of their sockets. The cold was intense, and the icicles on their noses and under their bellies jingled like beads or bugles. We were obliged to walk during the greater part of the way.

Having, however, arrived at Ingram's, we baited, and with as little delay as possible proceeded onwards on our journey. With equal toil and difficulty the horses completed eleven miles more to Maclachlan's, the whole of which distance I was obliged to walk by the side of the sleigh. We baited again, and the driver, anxious to proceed notwithstanding the fatigue of the horses, brought them out once more. They very soon became quite knocked up, it was perfectly dark, and the cold intense. Although we had only travelled four miles from the last house, we had been for many hours during the day exposed to the weather, and after all, having started before sun-rise, had only completed twenty-five miles. However, by good fortune, a light appeared at a little distance from the road, which we found proceeded from a log-house, where the driver proposed to remain for the night. With all the

feelings of cold and dreariness that surrounded
us, and leaving the man to settle and arrange
all matters of etiquette with the owner of the
house, I followed and submitted myself to his
arrangements.   But I need not have put myself to much uneasiness, for in that part of the
country matters of this sort are soon settled.
I was rather surprised to see the driver enter
the house quite as if it were his own.   He
hardly said "how do ye do" to the master and
mistress, who were quietly drinking their tea;
but, throwing a large log which he had
dragged in with him upon the fire, and taking
a key which was hanging upon a nail in the
wall without asking for it, he disappeared for
the purpose of putting up his horses.

I felt that I was in a private house, and
said some civil speech expressing myself obliged by being permitted to remain under the
roof for the night.   But I was quite at cross
purposes ; and I might just as well have re-
served my apologies for future occasions.   At
present I had quite enough to do to answer
the questions which were put to me about

myself and the " old country." I found I was a welcome guest, and as the fire blazed up prosperously, I looked at the boards in front of it as at my place of repose for the night; for the people had not a bed to give me.

As countries become more civilized, the social feeling is proportionably restrained; and hospitality and barbarism are, it is said, generally met with together. Still humanity is admirable, which, flowing from the heart, offers shelter to the stranger, who elsewhere might seek it in vain. The circumstances of the country induce a necessity for the exertion of hospitality; for in a climate so severe, and where houses of public entertainment are not everywhere to be met with, common consent establishes a reciprocity of accommodation, where to remain out of doors all night would be the cost of life. In fact, a man cannot be said to be master of his own house so as to exclude the visitors whom chance may throw in upon him. Sleeping without any other fastening than a latch to his door, a dozen strangers may enter one after another, who, dropping down to rest before the fire, take up their quarters for the night without the ceremony of asking leave of any body. The poorest person is not the least welcome, nor, in the exercise of hospitality, is any regard paid to condition and appearance. The people have enough to answer their own wants, and, as they are secluded from the world in a manner, are remunerated by the news they occasionally receive from the passing traveller; indeed it is a question, which of the two is the best off, the penniless guest or the host himself; who cannot, in his own house, walk across his bed-room after nine o'clock at night, without the risk of disturbing some great fellow stretched out and snoring before his fire, and who, if he happen to be trodden upon, will swear as loudly as if the whole house belonged to him.

My landlord and his wife were both extremely civil, good people. They had cows, pigs, and poultry, and all the requisites of a small farm; and finding by degrees, in the course of the evening, that my stock of provisions was expended, they thawed and set before me a frozen goose, which I thought excellent. They listened to me with great apparent satisfaction while I related to them the different little incidents of my journey, such as I thought would amuse them; and having in return for their goose filled them as full of news as I could, I prepared to stretch myself on the boards before the fire. With my feet towards it, I wrapped myself up in my buffalo skin, and, laying my head upon a log of maple, I listened to the crackling of the large pieces of wood freshly heaped upon it, till I fell sound asleep. I did not awake till the morning; and how my landlord and his wife got to bed, although they slept in the same room, I really cannot tell. In the morning I had seated myself on my wooden pillow before the happy pair had arisen; but the ceremonies of the toilet were quickly performed by all parties, and a warm breakfast completed the preparations for the ensuing day's journey.

January 3d. — It was scarcely daylight when we were quite ready to proceed ; for the snow lay so deep on the ground, and the difficulty of getting forward was consequently so great as to make our progress quite uncertain. Sitting in the sleigh was now out of the question; the horses had quite enough to do to draw it when empty. Proceeding at a rate of not more than three miles an hour, the driver led the horses ten miles to Phillips's, which house is situated on the banks of the river. Having baited, we got on fourteen miles more, walking all the way, and arrived at a house, where, as it was now quite dark, we put up for the night. I got here a very comfortable clean bed. We performed the last three miles of the stage on the ice of the river, which was tolerably clear of snow. About a couple of hours before sunset, a considerable change took place in the weather, which, during the whole time since I had left Fredericton, had been intensely cold. It became suddenly mild, and before nine o'clock a rapid thaw set in, attended with rain and sleet; the rain, however, lasted for a very short time, and was succeeded by a thick fall of snow. This event seemed entirely to mar our further progress; for labour greater than the poor animals had already encountered did not appear practicable. Should the worst come to the worst, I was now only eighteen miles from Presque Isle, and expected every hour to fall in with the postmen. I felt rather anxious on this head, as I did not much like to trust to an Indian as a guide.

January 4th.—At daylight this morning the snow was still falling in great abundance, so that, what with the state of the weather and of the horses, our doom seemed fixed for this day at least; we therefore voted expedient what was unavoidable, and granted the poor animals a boon which it was not in our power to withhold from them,—that of a day's rest. Bad as the travelling was, it was better than remaining in our present quarters; for neither quiet nor comfort being within my reach, I found myself more satisfied with fatigue. The driver had established himself

by the side of the fire, where, by the aid of
his pipe and a bottle of rum, which he had
not forgotten to bring with him, he at first
began to listen to the conversation of the other
persons in the room, and by degrees to become
a talker himself, till he made himself perfectly
happy and comfortable; nor did he seem to
care at all which way the world went. There
were four or five men in the small room we
were in, some belonging to the house, and
others weather-bound like ourselves; and these
fellows had all got the best places at the fire,
drinking and smoking. As their voices became elevated, unfortunately the imagination
flagged, and they became a noisy set, from
whom there was neither entertainment nor information to be derived.

And so I had nothing to do, but listening
with anxiety to the howling of the wind, which
was blowing clouds of snow against the windows, to reflect what a forlorn place I was in.
I determined to run all risks, by leaving it at
daylight the next morning. I walked backwards and forwards, and fidgeted,—all to no

purpose. Every time I opened the door of the house to look out to windward, I was greeted by the execrations of the whole crew within,— perhaps not without reason, for the wind, while it made balloons of the women's petticoats, filled the room with a whirlpool of snow, and as it took one's whole strength to close the door against it, it seemed every time that the weather was growing still worse and worse. But at last, about the middle of the day, things began to mend : it suddenly became brighter, the snow ceased to fall, and the change grew more and more evident, till the sun himself gladdened the scene with his presence; and, flying before him, the heavy full-charged snow clouds in rapid succession rolled away to leeward. As the sky grew clearer and clearer, all our countenances lightened up also; and I had not been long engaged in reading the congratulatory looks of the driver, who was now in a humour to be pleased with any thing and every thing, when the door opened, and two men on foot, of a tempest-driven appearance, with their clothes

and caps covered with snow, having each a
pair of snow shoes slung at his back and a
large white leathern bag across his shoulder,
entered the room.   Waiting for a moment on
the threshold, they shook the loose snow off
their feet by striking the hinder part of the
calf of each leg with the great toe of the opposite foot very rapidly,—a Canadian fashion,
as common as making use of a mat in England, and which becomes so much a habit, that
the Indians never enter a room, even in summer, without going through the motion.

These men were received with evident marks
of cordiality by every one in the house, and I
discovered, to my great satisfaction, that they
were the identical persons I expected to meet
with,—the postmen in charge of the mail-bags
from Quebec, whom, on their return thither,
I had made up my mind to engage as guides.
They were both native French Canadians, one
having, to all appearance, a little—or not a little
—Indian blood in his veins, being, as is very
common in the country, crossed with the savage.
I lost no time in commencing a negociation,

which I completed by agreeing to give them fifteen pounds as guides from Presque Isle across
all that tract of country necessary to be traversed
in snow shoes; that is to say, along the course
of the river St. John's by the Madawaska
settlement and lake Tamasquatha to the shores
of the St. Lawrence; and they were to draw
my baggage on my two tobogins. As they
had no means of delivering over the mail bags
of which they were in charge, they proposed
the house of a Mr. Turner, at Presque Isle,
(which place was, as I have already observed,
eighteen miles distant,) as the point of ren-
dezvous. It was uncertain when they would
be able to arrive there, for it depended upon
their getting rid of the mail-bags. I had a
reasonable expectation of not being detained
long from the known powers of these men as
pedestrians. At all events, they had no
sooner completed the arrangement than they
prepared to quit the house, and, after having
lighted their pipes and taken a dram apiece,
they bid us all farewell, and proceeded on
their journey in high spirits, keeping up a

long light trot till out of sight. These matters being now well off my mind, and the weather appearing once more settled, the house, its inhabitants, and the prospects of my journey assumed " *couleur de rose.*"

January 5th.—When we started, at daylight in the morning, we found the country enveloped in a thick fog,—so dense, that we were unable to distinguish any object at more than twenty yards distance; at the same time it was so intensely cold, that our clothes were, in the space of an hour, frozen stiff with ice. I set out walking: though the state of the roads was better than could be expected, considering the quantity of snow which had fallen, and which lay lightly on the surface; still, however, the travelling was bad enough, so much so, that the horses fell several times during the stage, notwithstanding the extremely slow pace at which they proceeded. All these roads, or rather tracks, have been originally made by the simple operation of chopping down the trees with the axe, generally in the winter season, so that stumps are

left standing in the ground, and a considerable number of years elapse before they rot
and leave a hole. Sometimes the horses, in
going along, blundered over some of these
stumps barely covered with snow, so that
the bottom of the sleigh would have been
staved in had we been in it. Now and then
their fore feet sank in altogether, and the poor
animals would pitch forwards upon their noses;
they were so frosted and bespangled with hoar
and ice, that it would have been difficult to
say, ten yards off, what description of creatures
they were. How their driver got them back,
I do not know.

I had left off my shoes on leaving Fredericton, and had adopted mocassins instead.
Though I had felt great advantage from the
change in walking through the deep snow,
this day I experienced an inconvenience which
I had not anticipated; for the hard stumps
of the trees were in some places so treacher-
ously covered with snow, that I repeatedly
struck my toes against them so hard as to put
me to considerable pain; at this the driver

H

was much amused; for, said he, " Monsieur, we call dat in dis country, de dram." He contrived, by habit, to avoid such accidents. Within a few miles of Presque Isle, we came to some places where bullocks had been employed to break the road, and their tracks were visible where they had been driven backwards and forwards for that purpose.

It was quite dark when we came to the end of the day's journey, and I had had nothing to eat since daylight; so that I was rather exhausted when I arrived at an old crazy house, the residence of Mr. Turner. I begged for something to eat, and a few slices of fat pork fried up with chopped potatoes were set before me. I thought, at the time, that nothing I had ever eaten tasted so well; and the repast being very soon concluded, I began to look a little about me, and at the people in the apartment I was in. I was particularly amused with the appearance of Mr. Turner. My host was, I believe, an American,—a tall, withered, thin man, about sixty years of age, with extremely small legs and thighs, narrow

shoulders, long back, and as straight as a
ramrod. Innumerable short narrow wrinkles,
which crossed each other in every direction,
covered his face, which was all the same colour—as brown as a nut; and he had a very
small mouth, which was drawn in and pursed
up at the corners. His eyes were very little,
black, keen, and deep set in his head. He
hardly ever spoke; and I do not think, that
while I was in his house I ever saw him smile.
He was dressed in an old rusty black coat and
trowsers, both perfectly threadbare, and glazed
about the collar, cuffs, and knees with grease;
and he sat always in one posture and in one
place,—bolt upright on a hard wooden chair.
He seemed to me the picture of a man who,
from want of interest in the world, had fallen
into a state of apathy;—and yet that would
seem impossible, considering that Mr. Turner
was the chief diplomatist in these parts,—the
representative of the commissariat depart-
ment, charged with the duties of supplying
the garrison at Presque Isle,—a man of high
importance in his station, invested with local

authority, and in direct communication and correspondence with the higher powers at Quebec. Notwithstanding all this, the energies of Mr. Turner's body and mind were suffered to lie at rest; for the garrison consisted of a corporal and four privates, making in all five men, to supply whom with rations was nearly his whole and sole occupation; and so he had gradually sobered down into the quiet tranquil sort of person I found him. A daughter, a fine, handsome, bouncing girl under twenty, with sparkling black eyes and an animated countenance, seemed to bear testimony to days gone by, when affairs were somewhat more lively; but the contrast now was sufficiently striking; for without regarding her, any body, or any thing, he kept his place and attitude, sitting always close to the stove.

There was a small square hole in the centre of the door, (as there generally is in all Canada stoves,) made to open and shut with a slider as occasion requires: this he kept open for a purpose of his own; for by long practice he had acquired a knack of spitting through this little hole with such unerring certainty, by a particular sort of jerk through his front teeth, that he absolutely never missed his mark. This accomplishment was the more useful to him, as he was in the habit of profusely chewing tobacco,—all the care he seemed to have!—and he opened the door of the stove now and then, to see how the fire was going on.

I had been indebted to Miss Turner for my supper, and she had made arrangements to prepare an apartment for me in the house, to which when I retired I found I had made an exchange very much for the worse. The house was ill-built, and my room so miserably cold, that to sleep in it seemed a forlorn undertaking. Several panes of glass were cracked, and others were entirely out of the windows, while the ceiling and walls were also out of repair. They had no bed to offer me, and a hay paillasse was the substitute. This I drew as near to the chimney as I could, as soon as Miss Turner had consigned me to my meditations. Wrapping myself in my buffalo skin, I attempted to go to sleep; but that was quite impossible, and I never remember to have suffered so severely from the cold, while I was in the country, as on that night. I had no thermometer; but the temperature, I am sure, was some degrees below zero. On getting up in the night to mend the fire with the tongs, the iron froze to my fingers, so as to feel quite sticky,—an effect of cold I have subsequently experienced on several occasions. I passed a very miserable night, sometimes walking about the room and beating my sides with my arms, and then trying in vain to sleep by the fire.

January 6th.—It was no sooner daylight, than I left my room in search of the apartment where I had passed the evening, which was, owing to the power of the Canada stove, quite of another temperature. Mr. Turner and his daughter made their appearance, and breakfast was prepared. This refreshment, though great, was not sufficient to remove the degree of cold with which I was suffering, so I prepared myself for a walk on my snow shoes. I had heard no more of my guides since I had concluded my bargain with them; therefore was obliged to await with patience their arrival: nothing else would have induced me to remain so long at Presque Isle.

Mr. Turner had resumed his place on the wooden chair, and the morning was clear and frosty when I set out. My snow shoes were now more useful than ever, for their weight increased the labour of walking, and so restored what I had so much need of—warmth. As soon as I had tied them on, such was the dreary, desolate state of every thing around me, that I never felt more undetermined what course to pursue. The river St. John's, with a covering of four feet of snow on the ice, pursued its course through a ravine at a little distance from the house. The forest, on both sides of its banks, reached the water's edge; and a small square patch of cleared land was all that pointed out to the eye the dominion of Mr. Turner. I descended the bank and crossed the river, entering a little way into the forest. All was silence and solitude; animals and birds seemed to have deserted the country,—except the squirrel and the woodpecker, and these at times I could hear a long way off. The squirrel followed me as I went along, chattering and jumping from tree to tree among the branches;—a man of pleasure, eager in the pursuit of the novel and the curious!—while the woodpecker, like a steady man of business, hammered and rapped away, less easily allured from his daily occupation. I rested and listened. There was no wind; even these small sounds pervaded large regions of space; and, at intervals, the creaking of the old trees, and the heavy lumping fall of the clotted snow through the branches, rendered the contrast with animated nature still more dismal. I left the wood, and proceeded along the bed of the river, which was of considerable breadth; and here I walked for upwards of an hour, without seeing a track or footmark of any sort. Had I not known that I was within a short distance of a human dwelling, nothing that I then saw could have led me to conclude that such had been the case.

When I returned to the house, I found that the guides, whom I had engaged on the 4th, had arrived soon after my departure, having travelled a great part of the night; and they, Miss Turner, and my host, were about to sit down to a mess of fried pork and potatoes, then hissing and sputtering on the top of the stove. I was well prepared to join in the repast, and we all sat down together.—The society now seemed to be receiving a tone; and though Mr. Turner still persevered in not saying a word, his daughter's features had received a polish from her office of cooking, and her eyes had increased in brilliancy to no small degree of intensity. The guides were boisterous vulgar fellows, who joined loudly in the conversation, intruding upon every body with elbows and shoulders. I frequently withdrew my chair to make way for them; but found hints were thrown away upon men so nearly related to the aborigines of the country. They, in fact, knew no better, spoke bad French, were full of Gasconade, and, while they thus asserted a miserable independence, it was really curious to consider, that these fellows were not only my servants, but my slaves,—rather, my beasts of burden and draft, for they were the next morning to harness themselves and draw my baggage over the snow. With this reflection, I left them to enjoy their prerogative of independence, and became a listener as well as Mr. Turner, whose apathy nothing could disturb, and he still shewed no other symptoms of animation than to spit into the fire through the little square hole, and now and then to rout about in his pocket to find his tobacco box.

The day flagged heavily, and night at last came, when, profiting by past experience, I lay down on the boards before the Canada stove, having taken early possession of what I fancied to be the warmest position for the night. The rest very soon followed my example; Mr. Turner and his daughter retired to their several apartments; and at eight o'clock all the house was quiet.

January 7th.—A delay on the part of one of the Canadians prevented our setting forward this day on our journey; and I never remember to have been so anxious to get out of any house I ever was in in my life, as this. To be impatient was of no avail. The half-bred Canadian had disappeared on a visit to his dam Sycorax, or on some other expedition in the neighbourhood, no matter to me whither: we could not go without him, and that settled the question. Late in the evening, however, he returned, with a small bag of provisions he had been to fetch. He lifted up the latch, and, at the first glimpse of his ugly face, feeling all the joys of liberation, and heartily tired of being where I was, in the joy of my heart I exclaimed to myself, " *Sic me servavit Apollo!* "

JOURNEY FROM PRESQUE ISLE

TO RIVIERE DE CÁPE.

EARLY in the morning a large mess of fried pork and potatoes was sputtering on the stove, and the party speedily assembled to partake it. I was happy to find the diet agreed with me, seeing little chance of getting any thing else for some time to come. The tug of war had now arrived, and the guides set about busily to prepare for our march. They cut leathern thongs with their knives, tied knots with their teeth, over-hauled the snow shoes, mocassins, and tobogins, and very soon put every thing in perfect order. It required but little time to load the tobogins. All the small articles were put into the tobogin bags, the larger things were wrapped up in the blankets and buffalo skin, and then altogether they were laced round with cord, so compact and tight, and fastened to the tobogin, that no accident could possibly disturb them. When the tobogins were ready, the men took a broad strap of leather, of which they made a sort of collar, passing over the breast and shoulders, to which a rope being fixed, each man was ready in harness, and able to draw his load with his arms perfectly at liberty. Our snow shoes were now all on, and at nine o'clock in the morning we marched away in single file, following the leader.

We wended our way down the ravine towards the river St. John's, which we immediately crossed; and the ice, which I had walked upon the day before, fortunately with impunity, not being considered safe, we were obliged to pursue our course through the wood, in a line parallel with this river, where stumps of trees and fallen logs presented impediments which added to the difficulty of travelling at this the very beginning of our journey. And thus we proceeded about four miles before we were enabled to go upon the river. Besides myself and servant, three other travellers had joined our " caravan", from Mr.

Turner's. Our party, therefore, consisted of seven persons, all of whom, with the exception of the guides, were perfectly unaccustomed to walking on snow shoes. I had imagined that I was matched in a fair handicap with men who were each to pull a laden tobogin after him, and therefore it never entered into my imagination that these fellows would beat me in pace with such odds against them; but here I found my mistake, and saw plainly that the advantage of practice was far more than equivalent to the weight of draft of a little machine, which slipped lightly and easily over the level surface of the snow, and which but very slightly impedes the progress of persons accustomed to draw it. On these fellows walked, without looking at all to the rear, and we all followed in a string, the more extended the farther we went. Added to the weight of the snow shoes themselves, they became clogged with ice; for there was much water between the surface of the river and the snow, which froze immediately, and produced a most heavy incum-

brance. From the time we started (nine
o'clock in the morning) we continued to walk
incessantly till half-past four, the guides occasionally halting in order to collect the party
together, and allow time to break the ice
which adhered to the snow shoes, by beating it
off with short sticks with which we had all provided ourselves for the purpose. Our rate was
less than two miles an hour, although we laboured hard to proceed, so clogged and impeded were we by the weight of the snow
shoes.

We went on without meeting a single person over a tract presenting no change to the
eye; we had one uniform white expanse of
snow before us, and we were bounded on each
side by the heavy black wall of forest trees.
However, at last, at half-past four, the grateful appearance of a small patch of cleared land
was hailed with infinite gratification, and, one
after another, we all entered the small log-
house which was to be our place of rest for
the night. It was of the most simple contrivance; we were altogether in one room;

a fire composed of enormous logs blazed on the hearth, and a cord went across the ceiling, or more properly the roof, (for ceiling there was none,) above the fire. On this cord the mocassins and stockings of all the party, which were quite wet from the springs we had occasionally passed over, were suspended, and no one seemed to usurp more authority in the establishment than another. The host and his family took matters very quietly. Their furniture was such as could not be very readily destroyed, corresponding with the walls of the house, which consisted of entire pine logs, having the interstices filled up with mud and moss. Being arrived and under shelter, the state of rest from fatigue was most particularly grateful. As to comfort, I had the means of making myself dry and warm, so I was not at all the worse for my day's work, and could appreciate the homely fare which was preparing for me, consisting of salted pork and sliced potatoes.

We had travelled only ten miles, according to the computed distance from Mr. Turner's

at Presque Isle, but the measurements had
been taken from point to point, at a time when
the ice was perfectly sound, and were necessarily very much exceeded in a journey thus
undertaken at the very beginning of the season, when it was impossible to pursue the
nearest and most direct course; so that the
ground traversed, was a great deal more than
the measured distance, and, in fact, admitted
of no comparison with it. I had felt little inconvenience from the wet during the morning,
as it had hardly penetrated the coverings of
my feet and legs; but a very few minutes after
arriving in the house, the warmth of the fire
caused the glass slippers to thaw, and I became thoroughly soaked. Although the dwelling of a Canadian peasant may not deserve
much praise, too much cannot be said of his
fire. An enormous log, so big as to require
the strength of two or three men with levers
to bring it in, is laid at the back of the hearth,
and this the Canadians call the " bûche": a
large one lasts full forty-eight hours, and ours
this night was a brilliant specimen. So that

I

my lodging was at least good, and I slept soundly on the boards, wrapped up in my buffalo skin.

January 9th.—It was no sooner day-light than the room was replenished with tobacco smoke, which formed, the preceding evening, a cloud so dense as to render it difficult to distinguish a face across the apartment. I jumped up and found the guides anxious to proceed, so I got my breakfast as soon as I could, and that was with little delay enough, for a slice of pork toasted at the end of a fork was all I had any chance of procuring: nor had I any tea. On starting, we found that more snow had fallen in the night, which, although it lay soft and light, caused the walking to be, if any thing, worse than before. We passed over many places where water under the snow froze immediately from the intense cold, and encrusted our snow shoes with an additional heavy weight of ice. Particularly under the heel a large lump was continually forming a material impediment, causing one or other of the party to halt every

ten minutes, in order to get rid of it. At
every effort the foot felt as if chained to the
ground, such was the tug required to bring
along the laden snow shoe; and as the shores
of the river were now gradually widening,
the feeling of disappointment was added to
our labour by the deceptive idea of distance
created. The eye was unceasingly directed
towards some bluff point, which, after an
hour's hard fagging, seemed not much nearer
than before; such was the effect of the dark
colour of the trees, contrasted with the
whiteness of the snow. A powerful wind
opposed our progress, and one seemed separated by interminable space from headland
after headland, and gasping, as it were, under
a sort of spell-bound influence, such as a disturbed dream brings to the imagination.

We had nearly completed fourteen miles
to a small log-house, where we were to pass
the night, when my servant fell up to his
middle into an air hole, which the fresh snow
had covered over so deceptively, that had
there been a hundred more such in our path,

we had no means whatever of avoiding them.
Fortunately the hole was but small, so that
he supported himself by his arms till we
pulled him out, with no other injury than a
wetting, of which alone the consequences
would have been serious from the intense cold,
had we not immediately afterwards arrived at
the house.   After this occurrence, affairs
seemed to take a new turn: I had com-
pounded for a long and a hard walk over the
ice, but had not thought much about tumbling
into holes; and as to measures of precaution,
reason went to convince me that it was to no
purpose to think about them, and quite as well
to leave the matter to chance; hoping for a
ducking rather than a drowning, should it ever
be my own lot to break in.   We passed the evening much the same as that of the day before,
for the guides smoked tobacco, together with
some other people, settlers in the vicinity,
who had temporarily added to our numbers.

One of these entered into conversation with
me, and requested me to take charge of a
letter to his friends, for his relations lived (he

told me) in the town of Ayr, in Scotland; and whether it was that his letter had miscarried, or from other causes, he could not say, but he had heard no tidings of them for a very long time. I readily undertook to take care of his letter, which the poor man immediately set about to prepare; but the way he commenced operations was too ludicrous to allow me to look on without being amused at the difficulties he had to contend with. He had seated himself on the ground in a corner of the room; his desk was a plate supported on his knees; his paper was as bad as well could be; his ink newly thawed and quite pale; his pen, pulled out of a wild goose's tail, was oily; his own hand was as hard as the bark of a tree, and his broad black thumb had been smashed by the blow of a hammer or an axe, and had no sort of bend in it. Yet, with such odds against him, he produced a folded epistle, of which I took charge and subsequently delivered to its address.

The difficulties attending the interchange of letters, between settlers in the colonies and their friends at home, are well worthy the attention of those desirous to promote emigration. The greater the facility of correspondence, the more the stimulus to individual adventure receives strength. Epistolary intercourse being kept up, the objections to foreign residence more resemble prejudices : withheld or delayed, they become solid, undeniable objections, and then it is that an emigrant may be considered really an exile.

January 10th. — When we started this morning the light was just beginning to dawn, and we had a heavy day's work before us, before we could arrive at any habitation; however, there was no remedy, but to push on with the rest. The guides to-day seemed particularly considerate, and, as if to give us every assistance, instead of driving recklessly on a-head, as they had been used to do, leaving us to follow as well as we could, and grumbling whenever they halted to collect the party, they now slackened their pace with great apparent good humour, and we all went on close together. However, we had not travelled more than half an hour, before they proposed that we should all walk first by turns. And their object by this arrangement clearly was, in case any of us should break in through the ice, to give us, with themselves, a fair chance of a preference. This was reasonable enough, and although they had undertaken to be our guides, we could make no objection so far to become theirs; and so it was settled that we were to exchange places every half hour. The labour was a good deal increased by being the first to break the way, and one thought of nothing else but being relieved from the task. The snow shoe makes a large track, so that the second man has a surface to walk upon which has been pressed down by the first, who, of course, has by far the hardest work of all.

And so we fagged on, careless of consequences; for the depth of the snow upon the bed of the river made it quite impossible to pick our way. Our guides prescribed the course from point to point, according to their notion of the safety of the ice, and the line

being once determined on, we had only to advance straight forward and trust altogether to
good luck. Long circuitous paths became
thus indispensable, and the danger of breaking
in after all certainly was not trifling. In the
mean time we were progressing heavily and
slowly, hardly saying a word to each other,
except when, at the expiration of each half
hour, it became necessary to exchange places
with the leading man. And this was not all,
for the clouds which had been all the morning unusually dark and lowering, seemed to
bear strong indications of an approaching
snow storm. At this juncture one of the
party, a strong, and apparently athletic young
man, began to complain of lameness in his
knee, which had swollen and had become very
painful. Still, however, we went on, and it
grew darker and darker, till a heavy fall of
snow, driven by a powerful wind, came sweeping along the desert track directly in our
teeth ; so that, what with general fatigue, and
the unaccustomed position of the body in the
snow shoes, I hardly could bear up and stand

against it.   The dreary howling of the tempest over the wide waste of snow rendered the scene even still more desolate; and with the unmitigated prospect before us of cold and hunger, our party plodded on in sullen silence, each, in his own mind, well aware that it was utterly impracticable to reach that night the place of our destination.

But, in spite of every obstacle, the strength of the two Canadians was astonishing; with bodies bent forward, and leaning on their collar, on they marched, drawing the tobogins after them, with a firm, indefatigable step; and we had all walked a little more than seven hours, when the snow storm had increased to such a pitch of violence, that it seemed impossible for any human creature to withstand it: it bid defiance even to their most extraordinary exertions.   The wind now blew a hurricane.   We were unable to see each other at a greater distance than ten yards, and the drift gave an appearance to the surface of snow we were passing over, like that of an agitated sea.   Wheeled round every now and then by the wind, we were enveloped in clouds so dense, that a strong sense of suffocation was absolutely produced. We all halted : the Canadians admitted that farther progress was impossible; but the friendly shelter of the forest was at hand, and the pines waved their dark branches in token of an asylum.—We turned our shoulders to the blast, and comfortless and weather beaten sought our refuge. The scene, though changed, was still not without interest ; the frequent crashes of falling trees, and the cracking of their vast limbs as they rocked and writhed in the tempest, created awful and impressive sounds; but it was no time to be idle : warmth and shelter were objects connected with life itself, and the Canadians immediately commenced the vigorous application of their resources. By means of their small light axes, a good sized maple tree was in a very few minutes levelled with the earth, and in the mean time we cleared of snow a square spot of ground, with large pieces of bark ripped from the fallen trees. The fibrous bark of the white cedar, previously rubbed to powder between the hands, was ignited, and blowing upon this, a flame was produced. This being fed, first by the silky peelings of the birch bark, and then by the bark itself, the oily and bituminous matter burst forth into full action, and a splendid fire raised its flames and smoke amidst a pile of huge logs, to which one and all of us were constantly and eagerly contributing.

Having raised a covering of spruce boughs above our heads, to serve as a partial defence from the snow, which was still falling in great abundance, we sat down, turning our feet to the fire, making the most of what was, under circumstances, a source of real consolation. We enjoyed absolute rest! One side of our square was bounded by a huge tree, which lay stretched across it. Against this our fire was made; and on the opposite side towards which I had turned my back, another very large one was growing, and into this latter, being old and decayed, I had by degrees worked my way, and it formed an admirable shelter. The snow was banked up on all sides nearly five feet high, like a white wall; and it resolutely maintained its position, not an atom yielding to the fierce crackling fire which blazed up close against it.

The Canadians were soon busily employed cooking broth in a saucepan, for they had provided themselves much better with provisions than I had. I had relied upon being able to put up with the fare I might meet with, not taking into consideration the want of traffic, and distance from the civilized parts of the province ; owing to which, the scanty provision of the inhabitants could not allow them to minister to the wants of others, although they might be provided with a sufficiency for themselves. And I now saw the guides pulling fresh meat out of the soup with their fingers, and sharing it liberally with my servant, whom they had admitted into their mess. The poor fellows seeing that I had nothing but a piece of salted pork, which I had toasted at the fire on a stick, offered me a share of their supper, but this I felt myself bound to decline. My servant had fewer

scruples, and consequently fared better.   In
return for their intentions I gave them a good
allowance of whiskey, which added to their
comfort and increased their mirth.   One by
one they lighted their tobacco pipes, and continued to smoke ; till, dropping off by degrees,
the whole party at last lay stretched out snoring before me.

Large flakes of snow continued to fall,
and heavy clots dropped occasionally upon the
ground.   Our enormous fire had the effect of
making me so comfortably warm, that I had
deferred the use of my buffalo skin till I lay
down to sleep, and were it not for the volumes
of smoke with which I was at times disturbed,
and the pieces of fire which burnt holes in
my clothes wherever they happened to fall,
my lodging would have been, under circumstances, truly agreeable.   I sat for some time,
with a blanket thrown over my shoulders, in
silent contemplation of a scene alike remarkable to me for its novelty and its dreariness.

The flames rose brilliantly, the sleeping
figures of the men were covered with snow, the

wind whistled wildly through the trees, whose majestic forms overshadowed us on every side, and our fire, while it shed the light of day on the immediately surrounding objects, diffused a deeper gloom over the farther recesses of the forest. And thus I remained without any inclination to sleep, till it was near midnight. A solemn impression, not to be called melancholy, weighed heavily upon me. The satisfaction with which I regarded the fatigue which had gone by, was hardly sufficient to inspire confidence as to what was to come; and this reflection it was, perhaps, that gave a colour to my thoughts at once serious and pleasing. Distant scenes were brought to my recollection, and I mused on past gone times, till my eyes became involuntarily attracted by the filmy, wandering, leaves of fire, which, ascending lightly over the tops of the trees, for a moment rivalled in brightness the absent stars, and then—vanished for ever! * * * I became overpowered with sleep, and, wrapping my buffalo skin around me, sank down to enjoy for several hours sound and uninter-

rupted repose.   I slept heartily till day-light,
when I awoke feeling excessively cold, and
found the whole party sitting up.   The snow
had ceased to fall, the sky had brightened,
and intense frost had set in.   The guides
were busy in preparation, and anxious to move
on.

January 11th.—Having breakfasted pre-
cisely as I had supped the night before, I was
soon, together with the rest, under weigh.   On
beginning to move I found my limbs stiff
with cold, and my ancles especially felt very
unpleasantly.   The day broke with a clear
sun, and the uneven ridges of drift which lay
in our path diversified our walk with a proportion of hill and dale.   Nothing could equal
the sparkling whiteness of the snow, disposed
as it was (as the sun mounted in the sky) in
every form and figure.   As I passed over its
surface, supported by my snow shoes, in some
places where it lay from ten to twenty feet
deep, there was a vivid novelty in the scene
which aroused the exhausted spirits, while the
cheering influence of the sun gave a new tone

and elasticity to the wearied limbs. We had walked for six hours, when we arrived at Salmon river, a distance of twenty-two miles from the house at which we had last slept. My limbs felt uneasy and I was restless. Our host was a veteran soldier, whose allotment of land was, as he told us, 105 acres. Towards the evening the weather changed to a thaw, with a sleet nearly amounting to rain, but, before nine o'clock, the wind chopped round again to the NW., and the frost set in again as severely as before.

January 12th.—Early in the morning we proceeded along the bed of the river to the Grand Falls; the ice all the way being extremely dangerous, not only from the effect of adjacent springs, but from the rapidity of the current, which in this part is very great. One of our guides this day met with a serious ducking: the ice broke in under him, and he fell into the water. The day was intensely cold, not only with a severe frost, but a keen piercing wind; and we were a considerable distance from any house. We were immediately

summoned to make the best of our way
to the bank of the river, where we all as-
sisted to kindle a fire; but, in spite of our
best activity, the man's feet were a little
frost-bitten before he had the benefit of it.
At a moderate distance from it, his companion rubbed them with snow till the circulation returned; and, in a little more than half
an hour, he was able to proceed without further injury. We pursued our way with the
utmost caution, the state of the ice being
more and more precarious, until we arrived
at a track, which, leaving the river, proceeded
up a steep acclivity, where we found ourselves,
after a walk of four hours, at the house of a
serjeant stationed at the Grand Falls, where,
as at Presque Isle, there was a small military
establishment kept up for the sake of the
communication. As it was about noon when
I arrived, I immediately got my dinner, and
was treated to the old fare of salted pork and
sliced potatoes,—a repast which had, at least,
the advantage of occupying little time; and as
I was anxious to see the Grand Falls, situated

K

about a mile and a half from the house, I put on my snow shoes, and, accompanied by the serjeant, proceeded on the way towards them.

On arriving at them I was amply remunerated for my trouble, by the magnificence of the spectacle ; not that the fall was on such a scale of grandeur as of itself to excite wonder, for it is not larger, perhaps, than the fall of Foyers, in the neighbourhood of Inverness, in Scotland ; but the garb of winter gave a character to its features unusually brilliant and pleasing ; for the vaporous mist which arose from it, as from all cascades of any degree of magnitude, was so increased by the intense cold,— the condensation was so extremely rapid,— that it is difficult to describe the effect it produced. Volumes of cloud rushed upwards, propelled from the abyss with most extraordinary force, so as nearly to resemble the escape of steam from the valve of an engine. The cascade was bounded on each side by craggy rocks disposed in huge disjointed fragments, and the tops of them were covered with snow, which had been affected by the

action of the spray in a singular manner, and
had received, by the constant impression of
its finer particles, an appearance exactly resembling that of sculptured marble.   The
dead whiteness of the snow had been changed
to a yellowish tinge, and it seemed like fleeces
of wool hanging over the rocks as drapery,
and arranged in the softest and most elegant
foldings.   The more distant the more soft
they became, and all were fringed at the base
with icicles; some of these, especially those
the nearest to the cataract, were of an enormous size.   The boughs of the trees also in
the vicinity were laden with small ones, like
beads of crystal; and altogether they reflected
the prismatic rays of the sun with magnificent
splendour.

The scene was charming; for the day,
though piercingly cold, was particularly bright,
and a clear dark-blue sky enlivened the whole
to a great degree.   One gazed with delight
as upon fairy grottoes and the works of magic.
Without snow shoes it would have been impossible to approach; and, as it was, I do

not know whether I stood upon snow supported upon the rocks, or clinging together by adhesion between the clefts. But this consideration presented itself to me only after I had been fully contented and gratified with the spectacle, and found myself standing in an advanced position, where I was hailed by the serjeant. I was very glad to get back, retracing my steps with great caution, and I fancied several times, that the snow felt much softer than it ought to be. I returned to the serjeant's house, where I lay down on the boards before the fire as soon as I arrived, in order to get as much rest as I could; for I was uneasy at the thoughts of the *mal à raquette*, which I feared, from the aching sensation about my ancles and insteps, I should not be able to escape.

January 13th.—We left the serjeant's house very early in the morning, which broke clear and cold. We walked a little more than two miles, and then came upon the river, along which we pursued our track. Not a particle of a cloud was to be seen, and that morning's

walk exhibited a loveliness of nature peculiar
to the Canadian climate, and sufficient to dissipate every sensation of pain and weariness;
a rare combination of frost and sunshine, such
as, without being seen and felt, can hardly be
imagined. The wind was hushed to perfect
stillness, and, as we walked along, our hair,
our seven days' beards, and the edges of our
caps, our eyebrows and even our eyelashes,
were as white as a powdering of snow could
make them. In the meantime, the warmth
of the sun gave a sensation of peculiar purity
to the air.

We continued all the way on the river, till
we had completed fifteen miles from the serjeant's house where we had slept, and had
arrived at the Grande Rivière. We were
now at the Madawaska settlement, composed
altogether of French Canadians; a narrow
strip of a village, where we sought the house
of an aubergiste, Rouen Croix, where I was
gratified and surprised to find I was to be
treated to a bed. Being perfectly lame, I
was delighted to hear, that I had done with

the snow shoes, at least for a day or two, and that for twenty-one miles the snow was sufficiently beaten to bear a horse and sleigh, which were to be had in the village. I of course lost no time in engaging one; and, considering the state of extreme necessity I was under, it is worthy of remark, that I found no inclination in the owner to cheat me. I agreed to pay fifteen shillings for the twenty-one miles,—a sum by no means exorbitant in the state of the road. I was much refreshed by a good mess of soup, with the meat in it, besides other ingredients I did not stop to inquire about: with all (sundry pieces of packthread excepted) I was perfectly well satisfied, for I was well persuaded of the possibility of faring much worse.

January 14th.—When the driver made his appearance with the sleigh, I found it to be of a different construction from any I had hitherto seen, and better calculated to pass over deep snow. It was, indeed, nothing more than a wooden box, having the runners or sliders so low, that the vehicle was dragged

along as much on its own bottom as upon
them. The snow was so deep, that it was
quite as much as the horse could do to get on,
stumbling and floundering at every step, while
the driver, with my servant, walked by the
side of the sleigh, driving with long reins.
The whole apparatus was so bad, that I would
ten times rather have walked; but I had
hopes of recovering from my lameness by rest,
and would have submitted to any inconvenience for the sake of being able to start
sound once more. Certainly I was in a helpless condition, and the roads within the limits
of this small settlement were so partially
broken, that the sleigh was overturned five or
six times in the course of the morning, when
I lay still and suffered myself to be righted
together with the vehicle each time, as the
shortest way, lame as I was, of helping myself. After all, it was a tedious slow drive,
and I should have been overturned much of-
tener if the driver's strength had not been
frequently applied on one side of the sleigh
to prevent it.

The twenty-one miles were at last accomplished, and we arrived at the house of an aubergiste, where the only spare room was already full of people; so that we were obliged to apply elsewhere, and were finally received into the house of an inhabitant, David Dufour, where two travellers had already established themselves. The room was exceedingly small, but there was no other, and this was to contain these two persons, ourselves, and the host and his family. The latter consisted of a wife and six children, all of whom were dreadfully afflicted with the hooping cough. As I was provided with some good mutton broth, I had not much to complain of till night; but then the crying and coughing of the poor children was very bad indeed. The noise, however, did not deprive me of sleep; and I awoke in the morning refreshed and even eager to undertake the day's journey.

January 15th.—A party of persons had collected for the purpose of proceeding with our guides towards Quebec; and so we all started together. It was with very great satisfaction, that I now saw my snow shoes tied fast on the outside of the baggage on the tobogin, having suffered so much by their weight; however, I very soon found, that the relief had come a little too late, for I was completely lame, and could not move a step without considerable pain. I contrived, notwithstanding, to keep up tolerably well with the party to the end of the day's journey, which was twenty-four miles. About a mile from the house where I slept we took our leave of the St. John's river, upon which we had travelled for so many miles, and, turning to our right, pursued our course along the Madawaska river, which empties itself here into the former.

The picture of our caravan was now totally changed. A dozen persons of various descriptions had joined our party, some at the end and some at the beginning of their respective journeys. They pelted each other with snowballs, and sang and whistled, smoking and hallooing. A few were hobbling and limping, being quite sick of walking, and fit for no sort of fun whatever. The guides had procured dogs to draw the tobogins, and several of these great creatures, from the coasts of Labrador and Newfoundland, were loose and followed in our train. The noise of the party frightened a Caraboo deer from his lair, and urged him, unfortunately for himself, to cross over the ice of the river just in front of us. Immediately there was a general hullabaloo, and men and dogs all at once gave chase. I quite forgot I was lame, and made a tolerable run too, and to my surprise found that the dogs had come up with their game, which had entangled himself by the horns in the branches of a fallen tree. There they pinned him, till one of the Canadians despatched him with his axe; and we had one of his haunches the same night cut into steaks for supper, which, although tough, were well-flavoured.

Although we had proceeded the whole of the morning without snow shoes, it was, nevertheless, extremely bad walking. The traffic in the neighbourhood of the settlement had caused a beaten track to be made; but the snow lay very deep on the ice, so that of necessity men in snow shoes had been the first to pass along it, until, pressed by their feet, it had by degrees assumed a surface capable of bearing people without them.   Still it was so soft, that the foot very frequently sank in deep enough to occasion a tumble.   Every man walked on as fast as he could, without taking any account of his neighbour; so that the fatigue of keeping up with the party was not a little increased by running to make up the lost way.   But any thing was better than having snow shoes tied to one's feet!   Having now walked twenty-four miles, we put up for the night in the house of a veteran soldier, who had received his allotment of land on the line of communication.

January 16th. — Our party had dispersed themselves during the night in other houses in the neighbourhood; but at an early hour they had all collected themselves in readiness to proceed.   We had a journey of twenty-one miles this day before us, and I was now so very lame as to make it a serious undertaking. We had, besides, two days more to travel on foot, before we could by possibility meet with any sort of vehicle. The consideration of a speedy end of the journey was a great inducement to proceed, and I determined to go on as long as I could. Our first six miles was along the ice of the Madawaska river; when, the ice being considered unsafe, the track frequently turned off into the forest along the bank. Having passed the head of the river, we came to Lake Tamasquatha, which is about fifteen miles long and from three to six broad. Our track lay over this lake, and we immediately went upon the ice and found the travelling much worse than on the river; for the wind blew violently against us, and it was as much as ever I could do to keep within any reasonable distance of the guides. We all followed one after another, while the foremost men almost vanished from the sight, and appeared like little black dots on the wide waste of snow ahead. Some, however, were behind me as tired as I was, though I never took the pains to enquire about them. At last we arrived at the house of Mr. Long, situated at the extremity of Lake Tamasquatha, and on the banks of that *portage** which extends from thence to the high road to Quebec without any interruption of water communication.

I had no sooner arrived than I threw myself down on the boards under a full impression, that I should be quite unable to proceed the next day. We found a new set of travellers, who had established themselves in the house; and these being reinforced by our numbers, a confusion of tongues prevailed in our room which set at defiance all description. We had thirty-six persons in it, besides six or eight large dogs belonging to the tobogins. We were obliged to lie on the ground like so many pigs. My next neighbour was a major in the army, whom I never saw before and have never met since; he seemed more fatigued than I was, and did nothing but groan all night. The dogs disturbed us; for they

* *Portage* is a French Canadian word, signifying the land over which it becomes necessary *to carry* the loads from one river or lake to another.

ran about and trod upon us; they growled; and twice before the morning there was a battle royal among them, with the whole room up in arms to part them by throttling and biting the ends of their tails. What with the noise, and the shouting, and swearing in bad French, we were in a perfect uproar. For this κυνομαχία, the natural remedy, of course, would have been to turn the dogs out; but the masters would not allow it, as they were of too much use by far on a journey. The gabble of tongues, the smell of tobacco smoke, and the disturbance altogether, was really dreadful; and there was, besides, a truckle bed in the room, on which two women reposed,— the mistress of the house and her sister. These females were not silent; and, no matter who slept, some were sure to be awake and talking. I quite lost all my patience; sometimes I struck at the dogs as they galloped over me, and I shook one fellow by the collar till he roared, who in the scuffle had trodden on my lame ancles without remorse. The only satisfaction I had was to think, that the pain I was in would alone, without the noise, have been sufficient to keep me from sleeping.

January 17th. — At an early hour this morning we commenced our journey over the *portage*, and, after travelling the whole day, I arrived, in a state of extreme pain and fatigue, at the place where we were to pass the night. We crossed several ravines, and had to climb steep acclivities. Both my feet were now swollen to a great size, attended with inflammation so acute as to resemble exactly determined gout. The Canadians told me I had certainly got the *mal à raquette ;* whatever it might have been, I lay awake all night in the miserable log house where we had put up, thinking how unlucky I was to have arrived within nine miles of the end of my journey on foot, without being able to accomplish the little that remained.

January 18th.—Nine miles were now before me, and if I could complete that distance the journey was done. The usual preparations for departure had no sooner commenced, than

I felt it quite impossible to remain where I was, although I could scarcely stand upon my feet; but as my servant was still strong and able, I relied on his assistance and set forward. I never was put to so severe a trial in all my life. The exertion of walking, and the twists I met with in the holes made in the hard snow by the feet of former travellers, were absolute torture; so that now and then I was obliged to lie down for a few seconds in the snow to recover myself. The cold was so intense, that almost as soon as I was down I was obliged to get up again, and a piece of bread in my coat pocket was frozen nearly as hard as wood. My servant staid by me whenever I lay down on the snow, and helped me to rise, and to him I am indebted for performing the short distance of that day's journey. I was eight hours on the way; but at last reached the village of Rivière de Loup, where I entered a small public house in the true spirit of thankfulness at having accomplished an undertaking of which I had several times despaired. But I remained there a very

short time : I found that I was only six miles
from Rivière de Cape, where there was a
good inn, and that it was possible to procure
a conveyance to take me there.

Beset as I was with a set of dirty companions, I ordered a sleigh to be got ready immediately, into which I made a last effort to
crawl, ready to endure any thing in the world
so that I could but free myself of my present
coterie. On arriving at Rivière de Cape, I was
gratified by the kindest attention from my
hostess, who placed before me the first comfortable meal I had seen for a long time. She
provided me with a good arm-chair, and many
other seasonable indulgencies; and it is re-
markable, that all pain left me that very evening. Never was a change more complete
brought about within a few short hours. To
think of both past and future created agreeable sensations, and the truth of "*Forsan et
hæc olim meminisse juvabit*" rushed forcibly
to my mind. The apartment and furniture
appeared elegant, my landlady lovely as Hebe,

L

my journey on foot was—thank Heaven!—
completed, and the refreshing silence of my
room added to the many comforts with which
I was now surrounded.

JOURNEY FROM RIVIERE DE CAPE

TO YORK, UPPER CANADA.

I WAS now on the high road to Quebec, where the river St. Lawrence breaks upon the view in splendid magnificence. A chain of mountains bounds the opposite side, and a long narrow island, called *l'Isle de Lièvre*, is situated mid-channel. The river is here twenty-one miles across, and appeared to be frozen over some miles from the shore. It is at this part quite straight, and the eye commands a reach of very considerable length. A post cariole (or small sleigh drawn by one horse) was to take me on my road to Quebec. I had made a good breakfast, had been kindly treated, had slept well, was relieved from the ragamuffins whose society I had participated so much too long, when I and my servant got into the vehicle. The road was well beaten and good; the horse started off at a sort of

shambling run,—a pace they all learn from
high calks and the continual habit of moving
through snow ; the bells jingled merrily ; the
sun shone bright with an intense frost ; and I
was not only so much recovered as to be perfectly free from pain, but the scene altogether
produced a buoyancy of spirits, the total reverse of the heavy-heartedness with which I
had only the day before, like an over-driven
ox, performed my journey. Although the
weather was by far too severe to make travelling in an open carriage at all agreeable, the
contrast made up for every thing. If it was
cold, I was well wrapped up ; my lameness
was getting better every hour, and I was sure
at least of being well housed.

The boy who drove me was a curiosity,—a
little wizened ape, hardly twelve years old ;
but he smoked, and swore, and cracked his
whip with all the grimace of a French pos-
tilion. A huge fur cap almost extinguished
his small face ; and he wore a close-bodied
coat, with a red worsted sash round his waist.
He had not proceeded far, when he stopped

at a house; and when I enquired what detained him, " C'est mon pipe, Monsieur!" Nor would he stir without " mon pipe"; and I was kept waiting several minutes while the people of the house were lighting it. At last he got it, and, giving a few hard whiffs, he cracked his whip, called the horse all the names he could think of, while he chattered away and grumbled in bad French, feeling his consequence hurt by the manner I had treated him. Changing sleighs at convenient distances, I posted this day sixty miles to Lislet. The charge was fivepence a mile : nothing was demanded for the driver, (which, I suppose, gave him the air of independence he assumed,) nor was there any other expense on the road. I found the delays in changing horses considerable.

The manner of driving is singular enough; for, instead of perpetually flipping the horse with the whip, as in England, they reserve it for greater occasions,—settling the balance of an account of errors by an unmerciful flogging, which lasts some seconds, and serves till the driver's patience is again exhausted. The horses are generally high couraged; but all seem crippled, owing to the manner in which they are shod, and the rough ground they have at times to travel upon.

Changing at short stages, I had travelled the whole of an intensely cold day, the sky having been quite clear and free from clouds. As evening came on, the glowing tints which suffused the bleak landscape were particularly beautiful,—such as a winter sunset in Canada can alone produce. The glaring sun became magnified as he touched the horizon. A deep fiery red was reflected from bright tin spires, and blazed from the glass windows of the scattered white houses in the distance. The snow sparkled with purple and varying prismatic colours; while large fragments of ice, scattered here and there, completed a picture of winter in all its intensity. I arrived at Lislet half frozen, having travelled some time after dark.

January 20th.—I posted this day fifty-one miles to Point Levi. A fall of snow in the night had made the roads very heavy, so that, although I started early in the morning, it was past ten at night when I arrived at the auberge,—an uncomfortable passage house, situated close to the banks of the river St. Lawrence, and opposite to the town of Quebec. The whole of the 111 miles I had travelled on this and the preceding day, was through a flat country, nearly parallel with the river. I had heard accounts by no means prepossessing of the mode of crossing over to Quebec, and of the state of the ice; but I was tired, and it was too late to make enquiries; so, as soon as I had procured a little refreshment, I went to bed, where, after I lay down, I could very plainly hear the roaring and splashing of the water.

January 21st.—In the morning, on looking out of my window, which commanded an immediate view of the Great St. Lawrence, there a mile and a half wide, I saw it frozen on each bank at least three or four hundred yards from the shore, and the channel filled with pieces of ice driven forward and backward by the eddies of an impetuous tide; these were rising one above another, twisting round and round, sinking, labouring, and heaving, by the action of a current running at the rate of seven knots an hour. Sometimes there was a space of clear water, wherein enormous flakes, of a superficies of three or four thousand square yards, would glide by; huge lumps, as big as a stage coach and all its passengers, would roll over and over, and tumble in various directions, now and then sinking altogether, and afterwards rising several yards a-head; large masses would meet, and drive against each other with a tremendous crash, piling flake upon flake, and presenting a most awful spectacle,—the more interesting, as it was my business to cross over that very day : and how that was to be done, I could not possibly, at the moment I have attempted to describe, determine. However, on holding a consultation with my host, I found, that the passage was certainly difficult, but, nevertheless, quite practicable ; that it would probably be attended with considerable delay, but that there was very little danger. Thus much was satisfactory, and I further understood, that slack water (it was now about half-tide) would be the time to attempt to get over. There was more ice in the river than had been for the two years last past, owing to a continuation of weather more than ordinarily severe, so that it was expected every day to set; and, whenever that took place, sleighs of all sorts would be able to drive across. Above all, I was recommended to lose no time in engaging a log canoe, unless I chose to wait for the chance of the ice setting.

Having no sort of wish to remain where I was, I found out a man who agreed to take me and my servant across for thirty shillings, after a hard bargain, in which he exaggerated the danger, and multiplied difficulties to suit his purpose. I met him by appointment on the bank of the river, about one o'clock, where he had his canoe in readiness to receive me, being attended by five Canadian boatmen, his comrades. The canoe was nothing more than fourteen or fifteen feet of an entire tree rounded at both ends alike, and hollowed by the adze. A piece of rope, six or eight feet long, was fixed at the head, and a similar piece at the stern. Each of the men carried an axe stuck in his sash, and a paddle in his hand; and thus equipped, they dragged the canoe from the shore along upon the ice, chopping away the last six or eight feet (where it became unsound) with their axes, till the head of the vessel was brought close above the water.

The tide was now nearly at the ebb, and its rapidity, of course, much abated; still the ice was continually in a state of violent motion, and presented a very formidable appearance. I now got into the canoe with my servant, and, according to the direction of the boatmen, who were chattering, arguing, and swearing on the subject of their plan of proceeding, we both sat down at the bottom of the canoe, in midships. And here we waited in readiness for a launch. A large flake floated by, leaving a clear channel of perhaps one hundred yards across, and this was the signal to begin. I had nothing to do but to sit still. " Tenez firme" they all cried at once, and without farther warning they pushed the canoe off the ice plump into the water with a splash. The fall was about two feet, and she was no sooner in than every one of the fellows, with uncommon activity, were on board and each in his place, paddling with eager haste, in order to avoid a large piece of ice which was bearing down hard upon us, and to gain a frozen surface right a-head. Succeeding in the attempt, they with equal adroitness jumped upon it, and seizing the rope which was fixed at the head of the canoe, drew her by main force out of the water, and, three at one side and three at the other, they pushed her along, running about a hundred and fifty yards across, till a second launch into clear water called again for the paddles. We were less fortunate in this than in the one preceding, for we were splashed all over, and the water almost immediately froze hard on our clothes. But we had not time to shake ourselves, for a large quantity of loose ice, which appeared just to have risen up from the bottom of the river, was bearing down upon us in a very formidable manner. The men paddled, and strained, and abused each other, but all would not do, and we were in a very few seconds hemmed in and jammed on both sides by a soft pulpy mass, together with which we were helplessly carried away by the current sidewise from the point we were endeavouring to reach. I could not help admiring the determination and address of the men at this moment; for they jumped out, above their knees in water, sometimes up to their hips, while they used their utmost strength to drag the canoe forward by the rope. Although the surface gave way continually under their feet, letting them down upon the large slabs of ice which were floating underneath, they managed, by pulling and hauling, and with their axes occasionally cutting and breaking away the obstructing blocks which stood in their way, to get free of all impediments, and gain once more a channel of clear water.

While this was going forward, it was extremely annoying to be perfectly helpless in the midst of so much bustle and energy, and when the fellows shouted " *branlez! sacre Dieu, branlez!*" they meant that we should rock the canoe from side to side as we sat, to prevent her freezing on to the ice; which disaster was only to be avoided by keeping her in continual motion.   If this had taken place, the consequences might have been serious, as the day was intensely cold, and we must have floated away with no very great chance of assistance. However, by the skill of the men we avoided it, and the thirty shillings were certainly fairly earned, for they were three or four minutes at this spell in the water, sometimes up to their knees, and now and then nearly up to their middle.   It seems almost incredible that men should be able to work at all upon ice so unsound as not to afford a surface capable of supporting the weight of the body; but on their part there seemed to be no sort of apprehension of absolute danger, owing to the vast thickness of the floating substance, a comparatively small part of which was, as they knew, that which appeared above the water. And there was invariably a lower stratum upon which they were received and supported as often as they sank in.

Such was the manner of making the passage across the river St. Lawrence, at the season of the year and under such circumstances as it happened to me to undertake it; and I have only to add, that the time occupied in going across was somewhat more than an hour, and that the varieties already cited followed each other in rapid succession, till the moment of our disembarkation at the opposite shore. At one time we were in clear water; the next moment struggling through congelated heaps of melted snow; then rapidly driven along over sheets of ice, and pushed over obstructing blocks which opposed our progress in ridges seven or eight feet high. The Canadians were, however, indefatigable. Every obstacle, so soon as encountered, was surmounted in a moment. Hard ice was hewn down with the hatchets. They were active as ants. All was energy, spring, and bustle. They were in the canoe and out of the canoe, paddling and cutting, pushing with the boat-hook, and hauling on the rope, all with instantaneous impulse, and appliance of strength in different ways and with the most effective success.

But notwithstanding all, it was with unmixed satisfaction that I found myself at last safely landed in the town of Quebec. Although I had nearly recovered from my lameness, the cold had made me very stiff, so that, in spite of the sun, the keen air had such an effect upon my limbs, that on getting out of the canoe I was scarcely able to move. The water with which I had been splashed had incrusted me in a coat of ice; and I was as much like an armadillo as a human being, when I crawled heavily up the steep, narrow, dirty street which leads from the lower to the upper town, bending my steps towards

Sturch's hotel, where I was shewn into the public room, well warmed by a Canada stove, and full of different sorts of people.

January 22d to 31st. The weather was all this time exceedingly severe, seldom above zero of Fahrenheit, and now and then several degrees below it. I was one day much amused by the effects of the cold upon the faces of the people in the streets when the wind blew exceedingly hard, and there was what the Canadians call a "podrè"*, which is a sprinkling of the finer particles of the snow from the tops of the houses; in clouds, which add a lively pang to the keenness of the frost. Indeed the effect is truly ludicrous. The moment a man happens to meet it, he stares aghast; the water bursts from his eyes; in one instant he shews his teeth (if he has any) to all the world; and his features become distorted and agonized. Nothing so miserable is to be seen, except the unfortunate dogs har-

* The Canadians have a way of their own of pronouncing French: thus, *la hache* they call *la hawche*, and so on.

nessed in small sleighs, and made to draw barrels of water (which, owing to the cold, smokes as if it were boiling) through the town.

The ice set in the St. Lawrence, and the " Pont" was formed on the 31st; an event which had not taken place for two years before. In a very few hours it was compactly wedged together, and covered with horses and sleighs in great numbers, and of the heaviest description. This may seem extraordinary, but it is a well-known fact, and very easily accounted for. For the masses of floating ice have previously attained a very great thickness, and are continuing to grow bigger every hour, as they are carried about in the stream by the current, the rapidity of which alone prevents their adhering long before. Sticking together at first by twos and threes, they jostle more and more every tide, till at last a general jam for a moment takes place; and a moment only does the business. The intense frost effects adhesion, and the water below splashing up between the interstices of the joints effectually fixes and rivets the whole. What from the thickness of the ice itself, and its being supported by the water, no weight can well be too great to put upon it. As soon as the ice has stopped, the river presents to the eye a wild and noble spectacle. The moment is naturally one of conflict and convulsion; and the throes and struggles of the impinging bodies are truly tremendous. Small islands of ice, pressed on every side till they give way, break in the middle, and, cracking into fragments, these become hurled one upon another in all sorts of grotesque forms; so that " when the hurley-burley's done", the whole surface of the river becomes covered, as it were, with little hills, houses, and villages. Objects that resemble all these are raised, as by the contrivance of magic, in the space of a few minutes. Some are of such considerable magnitude, that through the whole winter a circuitous track is taken to avoid them. And thus, although the inhabitants may immediately avail themselves of a passage, it is nevertheless necessary to break a road. Like any other desert track, a way must be cleared of impediments; however, as blocks of ice are easily cut through, much time is not required to put every thing to rights, and then crowds of persons flock to each side, eager to avail themselves of the first opportunity of crossing over.

The state of the river immediately before the setting of the ice is of course growing worse and worse every day, until the communication, as regards traffic, may be said to be impeded altogether. The forming of the pont, therefore, is hailed by the inhabitants of both sides with a joyous welcome: by the country people, owing to the prospect of bringing their produce readily to market; and by those of the town, from the hopes of a reduction in the prices of the articles, the natural consequence of the event.

The next point of my destination was the bay of Penetangushene, an outlet of Lake Huron, where it was the object of Government to establish a naval and military post. And as the place to which I was going was far removed in the woods, I made some preparations in the way of equipment. To this end, I purchased a good buffalo apron, in addition to the one I had before, and some articles of warm clothing. I also provided myself with powder and shot, having brought with me a good double-barrelled gun of Joseph Manton's, which had been dragged over the snow with the rest of my things on the tobogins. Thus accoutred, I felt quite ready to leave " the flaunting town", its split logs and hot stoves, to explore the ruder regions of the north-west.

February 1st. I posted to Rivière St. Jaquetiere, where I slept. The whole journey was extremely unpleasant, owing to the frequency of the cahôts, or trenches in the snow which lay across the road. The driver never pulled up his horses, but seemed to me to rattle over them with unnecessary rapidity, and at the imminent risk of breaking the sleigh.

February 2d. Posted to Trois Rivières.

February 3d. Posted to a small place within nine miles of Berthier.

February 4th. Posted to Montreal. As I intended to remain two or three days in the neighbourhood, I ordered a sleigh to take me the next morning to St. John's, a small town situated on the River Richelieu, between Lake Champlain and the River St. Lawrence, and distant twenty-seven miles from Montreal.

February 5th to 7th. Early in the morning of the 5th, I crossed the St. Lawrence in a sleigh, over a track as well beaten as any part of the streets; the large slabs of ice which had been removed, as well as heaps of snow, forming a wall on each side for a great part of the way. Turning to the right, the road continued along the bank for about three miles through the neat village of Prairèe; thence leaving the river, through a flat country, with inns at short intervals during the whole distance. Having then reached the river Richelieu, I arrived at St. John's, where I was hospitably received by Sir Thomas B——, under whose roof I remained until the morning of the 8th.

February 8th. Having returned to Montreal, I made arrangements to leave it the next day, and hired a sleigh with two horses to take me to Kingston. The appearance of the town was superior to that of Quebec; the equipages, especially, seemed much better appointed. Indeed, a well-built sleigh is a remarkably handsome vehicle. In shape like the Britska, of a dark colour relieved by scarlet, and covered with a profusion of rich black bear-skins, it has a striking effect in contrast with the pure white snow. The cold was this day more than commonly severe, and for the first time I perceived an effect of the low temperature, by no means unusual. My clothes, on taking them off, braces, waistcoat, &c. were so charged with electric fluid, that they crackled and snapped, producing sparks of fire in abundance. Even the comb which I passed through my hair created a similar effect.

February 9th. The driver of the sleigh made his appearance much later than he had promised, but was accompanied by the owner, who, by way of apology, told me that I had " the best span of horses in Montreal" for

my journey. A "span of horses" means a pair
driven abreast, and is one of the many American expressions current in this part of the
country. Indeed there is so little bar to the
communication along this part of the frontier,
that a great similarity consequently exists in
accent, manners, and general appearance between the inhabitants on both sides. The
road led occasionally along the bank, and now
and then on the bed of the river; which, owing to the very rapid current, was at parts
open in the middle, the channel being full of
small islands and rocks. Although the air
was piercingly cold, the sun shone forth with
great brilliancy, shewing signs of his increasing
power by the icicles which, in many warm and
sheltered situations, already fringed the eaves
of the houses. As I started late, I proceeded
no farther than Point Clair, where I put up
for the night. The landlord, a civil, bustling
man, replenished the fire, and was extremely
active. He said he " abhorred a bad fire",
and added, " I guess you'll like a glass of
sling after your cold drive." I discovered that

" sling" meant gin and water; so a glass of sling I took, and then went to bed.

February 10th. I travelled this day to Point Boudet, along the banks of the St. Lawrence, which here presents an interesting appearance—that of a mighty stream tearing its way through a channel which bears the strongest marks of some grand convulsion of nature. The foaming rapids, the heavy roaring of the waters, the huge slabs of ice ripped from the summits of the rocks, whose black desolate looking points formed a striking contrast with the overpowering whiteness of the snow;—all these were objects which irresistibly rivetted the attention. One beheld, as it were, with all the accompaniments of nature's sublimity, a contest of the two elements, wherein every inch of ground was furiously disputed. I afterwards passed these rapids on my journey back to Quebec, as I shall have occasion to describe. The inn at Point Boudet, where I put up for the night, was situated close on the bank of the river, and extremely tidy and comfortable.

February 11th. I proceeded this day to Cornwall, the weather being piercingly cold, with a bright sun. The same man, the servant of the owner of the sleigh, and a Scotchman, had driven me all the way from Montreal, and had hardly spoken a word the whole journey. But there was a bottle of "whaskey" which he kept under the seat, just within his reach, to which he now and then had recourse; and to-day, as the weather was cold, and the sun shone bright, he took a sup from time to time as he felt inclined; rather often, at every three or four miles perhaps,—till he began to fidget in his seat, and look round to me, as if he had at last got something to say. Therefore I asked him, *à-propos* to nothing, whether he thought he would be able to wear the kilt in Canada? " Na", said he, " the flies wad nap a body." I thought it was rather odd he should be thinking of flies at a time when the frost was biting so particularly sharp; but still he insisted upon it, that the flies, of the two, were the worst; and he suited the action to the word with such energy, that I could not doubt his veracity. I tried to engage him further in conversation, but that was impossible; for he was a Highlander, who spoke very little English when he left his own country, and he had been deprived of the small portion he then understood, by a residence of three years in Montreal, where his fellow-servants all spoke French. This had quite petrified his genius, and had spoiled him as a linguist altogether.

February 12th. It was remarkably cold when we started in the morning, and Dougall, whether owing to the effect of the whiskey the day before, or the melancholy appearance of the empty bottle, had relapsed into his former taciturnity. We travelled twenty-six miles along the bank of the river, and put up at an inn close to the water.

February 13th. I travelled twenty-two miles to Prescott, which is opposite to the American village of Ogdensburg. The river here was about half a mile wide, and frozen quite across. Some people at the inn were conversing on the subject of a lot of cattle which had been stolen, and they seemed to think it almost certain that they had been driven over the ice to the American side.

February 14th.   I travelled this day forty-two miles to Guananaqui, the road chiefly being out of sight of the river.   The weather was fine and clear, but so cold that the bay horses might have been mistaken for iron-grey, so powdered over were they with frost.

February 15th.   I had now twenty-four miles to proceed to Kingston, where I arrived early in the day.   I went to Thibodo's hotel; a large, cold, rambling house, the landlord of which was extremely attentive and civil.

February 16th.   As I had proposed to re-main a day or two at Kingston, I walked out on the ice to see the ship St. Lawrence, which was frozen in on all sides, quite hard and fast. Two seventy-fours, a frigate, and some gun-boats, were building in the dock-yard; and the above-named ship, (a three-decker, mount-ing 108 guns,) two brigs, and a sloop, were in a state of complete equipment.   At King-ston, the magnificence of the River St. Lawrence is particularly striking; for there, at a distance of several hundred miles from the sea, its expanding shores are seen tracing the limits of Lake Ontario. This magnificent fresh-water sea was frozen round the edges to an extent nearly as far as the eye could reach; the waters in the distance appearing like a black line in the horizon. The ship lay close to the town, with which a constant communication prevailed; as the officers and men were living on board just as if she had been at sea. Sleighs of all descriptions were driving round her; country vehicles, with things to sell, and others; and two ladies, who had driven themselves in a light sleigh drawn by a pony, were holding a conversation under her bows with a gentleman in a cap, which conversation, from its earnestness, might have imparted warmth enough to thaw the icicles which were hanging from the cabin windows. Numbers of people were on foot, and the snow was so trodden all round the ship, that it was really difficult to believe that a depth of water sufficient to float a three-decker was rolling under one's feet.

I found, on returning to my inn, that a ball was to be held in the house in the evening, and that my room had been determined on as one of the card-rooms. The assembly was held in a large corridor, or wide passage, with doors opening into little rooms on each side; of which latter, mine was one. The company, which was numerous, began to assemble very early, and soon commenced dancing with high glee. Pulling, romping, turning round and round, &c. was the order of the day, and the noise of tongues and feet " pretty considerable loud." What with the good spirits of the young ladies, and the good humour of the old ones, it was past three o'clock in the morning before the house was clear of its guests, when (as the beds had been all taken down for the occasion) I betook myself to a mattress which was spread for me on the floor.

February 17th. My landlord gave me for dinner some steaks of a moose-deer which had been killed in the neighbourhood; the meat was of a fine, wild flavour, although extremely coarse and tough.

February 18th to 22d. I left Kingston for York in a two-horse sleigh, which I had hired to take me thither. I was five days on the road, leaving ten miles for the last day's journey. The owner of the sleigh drove it, and was an honest-looking, healthy fellow, who wore a good coat, and had the appearance of a substantial yeoman. He told me that he had lived eighteen years on his present farm of two hundred acres, for which he had originally given three hundred dollars. The road during the journey was heavy, from a recent fall of snow; but the prospect was enlivened from time to time by views of Lake Ontario, along the shore of which we were travelling. There were several small lakes on the way. Among them, Rice Lake; so called from the wild rice which grows about it, and which is of a good quality enough, although small and of a brownish colour.

I met a couple of Indians dragging along a porcupine, which they had shot, by a long strip of bark, which served as a rope. The woods abounded with a large description of woodpecker, the size of a small fowl, with black bodies and scarlet heads, and called by the natives cocks of the wood.   When within ten miles of York, the cloud of condensed vapour proceeding from the Falls of Niagara, then perhaps forty miles distant, was distinctly visible.   The day was quite clear, without any other cloud in the sky.   On arriving at York, I was disappointed at the first sight of the capital of Upper Canada, which, although covering a large space of ground, was extremely straggling and irregular; and the inn was not by any means prepossessing.   I was shewn into a cold and dirty room, without any appearance of comfort, or even the cheering abundance of fire-wood I had been used lately everywhere to meet with.   They gave me a dry, black, and tasteless beef-steak for breakfast, which I finished as soon as I could, in my eagerness to get out of a disagreeable apartment, and make myself warm by exercise.

It being the season of the year when " the presents," as they are termed, are given to the Indians, these people were walking about the streets in crowds, all in their holiday apparel, and animated by the anticipation of what they were to receive—blankets, blue cloth, guns, powder and shot, &c. I could not help remarking the great difference between the Indians here and those in the provinces of Nova Scotia and New Brunswick. They were altogether a finer race of men, in countenance, carriage, and general appearance, more robust and athletic, and their faces broader and flatter, and of a deep copper colour. Streaks of red paint ornamented their cheeks; and what seemed the most fashionable bijou of their toilette, was a silver ring in the nose, with a bead of the same metal appending to it. There was a look of health about the women, which made many of them appear beautiful in spite of their flat noses. They had good teeth, and eyes of brilliant black, which received additional lustre from parallel streaks of red paint down their cheeks, which seemed, from their breadth, as if they had been laid on by the fore-finger. According to this method of rouging, art might fairly be said to enter into an honest competition with nature; for intermediate stripes of clear skin were always left as a fair sample of the original.

I remained in York till the 25th; during which time my stay was rendered agreeable by the friendly hospitality of Mr. C——, a gentleman of high respectability in the town. I understood, that the station of Penetangushene, whither I was going, was still an establishment quite new, and that some of the public officers were already there, and were hutted on the spot; but that no buildings of any sort had yet been erected; moreover, there was no house at all anywhere within thirty miles of the place. I was rallied on the nature of my future life and occupations, which, indeed, seemed likely to be sufficiently rural. I hardly knew sometimes what to think of it; but I bought a sack of potatoes and some rice, and prepared to start on the 25th, with Mr. C——, who, having a wish to see the new establishment, proposed to accompany me.

RESIDENCE IN THE WOODS.

On the 25th of February I left York, with Mr. C——, in a two-horse sleigh, on our way to Lake Huron. The snow was soft and the draft heavy ; however, the horses were good, and we travelled thirty miles to the village of Newmarket, (which lies about a mile out of the road on the right hand,) and arrived a little after dark. We were hospitably entertained by Mr. Peter Robinson, who provided us with a good supper and comfortable beds. Our host, as well as being a contractor with Government, was an agent of the North-west Company, and held, moreover, sundry provincial appointments. Added to this, he kept a shop in the house where we now were, which was plentifully stocked with all manner of commodities, particularly such as were suited to the wants and taste of the Indians : it was, in fact, the great mart to which all those in this part of the country resorted, to

furnish themselves with the different articles
of which they stood in need,—flour, cheese,
blue cloth, cottons, hardware, &c.; besides
guns, powder ånd shot, for the men, and all
sorts of millinery and ornament for the squaws,
such as flaring gown patterns, beads, and
rings for their noses.

February 26th.—We started very early
this morning; for, as it was our intention to
cross Lake Simcoe, we had every reason to
expect the ice would be in a bad state, and
the draft particularly heavy; for during the
last few days the sun had been extremely
powerful for the time of year, so that the
snow became always quite slushy after the
middle of the day. When we set out, the
morning was clear, and the frost had been
hard in the night; so that the snow was crisp
and slippery, and we had what might be called
an agreeable drive along a very good road to
Holland river, (which empties itself into Lake
Simcoe,) a distance of eleven miles. There
was a sort of public house established at the
spot where we had arrived, and which was

N 2

called the Landing, being the point from whence the river was considered navigable in the summer.   Here we baited the horses, giving them no more time than was absolutely necessary, owing to the unfavourable reports on the state of the ice in the lake, from which we were now about nine miles distant.   Holland river afforded to me a novel appearance : instead of the rocks and bluff headlands of the St. Lawrence, this little stream presented more peaceful and tranquil objects to the eye, and seemed to offer an assurance of calm and sequestered retreat.   The channel was frozen quite across ; narrow, with a profusion of reeds on each side ; the whole breadth being, perhaps, three or four hundred yards.   The sun shone bright, and the dry rattling flags, which the breeze set in motion, brought a more genial season to the recollection.   Our sleigh was soon brought out, and, being launched down the sedgy bank, the horses were put to ; and, having bid adieu to the last house we were likely to see for a distance of thirty-six miles, we pursued our course along the frozen surface of a stream where Fauns and Satyrs might have held their summer revels. But the lively green of spring soon faded in the imagination, opposed to the realities of winter. The snow lay deep on the ice, and, being melted by the sun, the draft was so exceedingly heavy, that the horses could proceed only at a foot's pace, and the sleigh sank so deep, that the water frequently reached the bottom of the carriage.

We had overtaken a party of English shipwrights at the public house we had just left, who were on the way to join the new station at Penetangushene Bay, whither we were going ; (they had been previously employed in building small boats for the navigation of the lake.) These men finding we were going thither also, followed in our train, and, as we travelled slow, they were enabled to keep up with us on foot. Pursuing the course of the river for about nine miles, the channel by rapid degrees became broader, till a wide sheet of snow appeared a-head, and we found ourselves upon the verge of Lake Simcoe.

Inclining to the left, we skirted it, cutting off its lower extremity, and making directly for Kempenfeldt Bay. We then bore about three or four miles up the bay, and put up at a log-house, which had been newly erected on the north bank, and stood almost close to the water's edge. This log-house had been built for the purpose of the communication to Penetan-gushene. It was very late when we arrived, and we had travelled thirty-six miles from Holland River, in all forty-seven miles that day. The driver was provided with food and clothing for the horses, which were scarcely defended from the weather by the miserable hut which was allotted to them as a stable. They were, I believe, the first pair of horses ever there. They were littered down with the boughs of the spruce-fir and a quantity of moss collected close to the spot. As for ourselves, our fare was equally simple. We made a roaring fire, and roasted some potatoes, which we eat with cold meat, with which we had taken care to provide ourselves; and this repast occupying but little time, the whole party, shipwrights

and all, each measured his length on the floor
before the fire. I now began to think I had
had enough of all this, and I did earnestly
long to be once more in some place, no matter
where, that I could call my home. However,
I fell asleep, and continued so some hours,
when I awoke, owing to the cold, and found
that one of my neighbours (having felt, I take
it for granted, cold too) had deprived me of
my buffalo skin, which was tightly wrapped
round him, while the fellow was snoring as
happily as if it belonged to him. The harder
I tugged, the harder he held on and snored;
and, as he was a thick-set, strong fellow, I
had the more difficulty to recover my property.
However, I jumped up, and, invoking the
spirit of Archimedes, I placed my foot on his
ribs to such advantage, that by one violent,
determined pull, I thoroughly uncased and
rolled him out on the floor.

February 27th.—We had already advanced
thirty-six miles from the house on the banks
of Holland River, which was the nearest human habitation worthy of bearing the name

between the spot where we were and the town of York; and the road we were now about to travel had been newly cut through the forest, so that it was as bad as it could well be. To assist the communication, however, a hut at the distance of twenty miles had been erected, where we intended to pass the night. The way was not better than we had anticipated,—if any thing, worse; so that we owed much to the assistance of the shipwrights, who were able auxiliaries: a dozen stout, good-humoured fellows, who helped us out of all our difficulties, and went on whistling and singing as if they were going to a fair. When we reached the hut, we found it nothing more than a few boughs raised up; of an oblong form, and having one of the long sides quite open to the weather. Fortunately there was but little wind, nor was the night very cold; so we made a large fire, and lay down in our clothes before it, as we had done the night before.

February 28th.—The road was still miserably bad, but with the assistance of the shipwrights we were enabled to reach Yeo River, a distance of ten miles. We were frequently obliged to take the horses out of the sleigh for two or three hundred yards together, while the men drew it over trees which had fallen across the road, roots of others which had not been removed, and other such impediments. When we reached the ice of Yeo River, we got on a great deal better, although, as at Holland River, the melted, slushy snow lay very deep. The banks were sedgy, and I observed frequent hillocks or mounds of snow thrown up, the habitation of the musquash, a species of large water-rat, having a long fur, which serves to make a good coarse felt for hats. We pursued our course till we came upon Gloucester Bay, and from thence we reached that of Penetangushene. We advanced up this bay about three miles, keeping the shore close on our left hand, till a small piece of cleared land, and the signs of human habitations, held forth to us the signal that the hour of rest was at last come.

Here, then, I was arrived! My residence

was in this very spot to be established, I could not tell for how long. As it was growing late, no time was to be lost : a column of smoke was to be seen ascending on the other side of the brow which overhung the beach, and to that I of course made my way. It was at three o'clock in the afternoon when I got out of the sleigh. The distance we had travelled in the day was, ten miles through the forest, and I think fifteen over the ice,—in all, twenty-five miles. On stepping out of the sleigh I was immediately wet through, owing to sinking half way up my legs in melted snow. The driver wishing to get back again the same evening to Yeo River, urged me to have my things taken out of the carriage, and was anxious to hurry me to make up my mind where I would have them deposited. All places were then alike ; so, desiring my servant to strew some spruce boughs on the snow a few yards within the forest, my baggage was placed upon them, and I left him to watch every thing, while I set forth towards the place where I had seen the smoke.

On entering the wood, I ascended a steep acclivity, which I had no sooner surmounted than I found myself amongst a parcel of small huts, made up of a few poles thatched over with spruce boughs, scattered here and there; and from two or three of these it was that the smoke issued. There was not such a thing as a log-house to be seen; but I observed, that one of the huts was rather better finished than the rest, and a farther distinction was allotted to it by a flag, which was placed upon the roof. It was evident, that none of them could have been long erected, the snow was so excessively deep, and the foot-marks so few; however, I made my way immediately towards the one with a flag, where I found Captain C——, of the navy; and I had no sooner entered and introduced myself, than I received a very cordial welcome. Captain C—— immediately afforded me the assistance of a couple of men to build me a hut; and, as it was necessary that it should be ready for me to sleep in the same night, I went back to the place where I had left my servant with the baggage. I told him where I would have the hut built; and, leaving him to superintend the works and remove the things, I returned to Captain C——, where I was regaled with a fine piece of boiled beef, which I was hungry enough to think excellent, though from its toughness it would hardly remain upon the fork. Captain P—— and Lieutenant E——, the other officers appointed to the establishment, had assembled at the Commodore's hut, and with them I remained till nearly seven o'clock, when I left the party to attend to my own affairs.

I had directed my hut to be erected on the summit of the brow which rose close from the bay; and when I returned to the spot I found my servant busily arranging my different articles of property in an edifice which, if not equal in splendour to the renowned palace of Aladdin, had been, at least, completed nearly in as little time. By the help of a few poles and cedar boughs, I had now, such as it was, a house of my own. There were at least two sides with a back part, and the front was open;

but a brilliant fire was blazing before it, big enough for the kitchen of the London Tavern, and in itself a world of comfort. The plan of the hut was not of my own contriving; it was such as local experience had determined upon, and of the following description: the front, where the fire was burning, was six feet high and eight feet broad; but the roof dipped towards the extreme end, which was only four feet high; and the length was exactly ten feet. The snow had been well cleared away from the bottom, and, being banked up, it helped to support the poles which formed the framework. A bundle of spruce boughs laid across the extreme end, with a sack of potatoes for my pillow, formed my bed; and if I had no door opposite, all the cold that got in necessarily passed through the fire and smoke. My baggage,—that is, a very small valise, a gun case, and some other little packages,—was easily disposed of within these narrow limits, and every thing was perfectly ready for my repose soon after it was dark. My servant I had got attached to the shipwrights' mess,—a noisy set of fellows, crammed altogether within a very small compass, and among them there were some singers, the sound of whose voices I used frequently to hear at night as I sat by myself.

March 1st.—Early this morning I provided myself with one of the workmen's axes, and began, by way of practice, to cut down trees; and there were many ways of turning this exercise to account. Of all things, I was the most anxious to keep the smoke out of my hut, and contrived various methods for the purpose, but unfortunately all without effect; so not succeeding in my first object, I set about making a bedstead. To this end I got four short, upright, forked pieces, upon which I placed poles across, tying them with strips of the bark of the bass tree, which I also wove in longwise and across, so as to make a tolerable substitute for a ticking, on which I might lie before the fire high and dry; on this I placed a mattress of spruce boughs, and altogether, with my buffalo skin for a covering, I rested comfortably. — The bass tree has a remarkably tough, stringy bark, which rips easily from the trunk, and is so strong and flexible, that it serves all common purposes of rope. The wood, at the same time, is almost as soft as a cabbage-stalk, and very white.

My time was so much occupied, that I was hardly sensible of the progress of the day, and I went on chopping and working till late in the afternoon. In the evening a gang of Canadian axe-men arrived from York to place themselves at my disposal; and this event, in the infant state of the establishment, was a great relief to me. Log-buildings were the first desiderata, to get ourselves under cover and to provide for the reception of stores, utensils, &c., such as in the uncertainty of events might at any future period arrive. These men hutted themselves before night, and some provisions, which had been brought with the party, were well thatched with cedar boughs for temporary security. My own comestibles were scanty; I generally relied upon being able to fare where others could, and had not provided myself nearly as well as

I might. My baggage, with the exception of the very small proportion brought with me, was at Halifax, to be forwarded by the first ships in the spring to Quebec; and as to seeing a particle of that, I might rest quite contented I should not before the middle of June at the soonest. With most articles of dress I could just now very well dispense; but I felt fortunate in having with me my double-barrelled gun, (which had been dragged over the snow on the tobogins,) and was quite ready for the birds of the country, so soon as ever they might make their appearance. None of the feathered tribe were yet to be seen, except some woodpeckers, and a few packs of snow birds, or " sna fools," as one of the shipwrights, who was a Scotchman, used to call them.

March 2nd.—Early in the morning operations for building log-houses were commenced. I decided at once on a spot for my own residence,—on the top of the brow, close above the bay; and all the trees which stood in my way I intended one by one to chop down, and so go on improving in beauty the front of my dwelling till the spring should embellish the ground with flowers and verdure. The logs for my house were soon ready, and the work began : the dimensions were twenty-one feet by eighteen.

As I was at work close to the water's edge, I found a large iron pot with three short legs. As it lay there without an owner, I felt the value of the services it was capable of performing, so desired my servant to remove it to my hut ; and his ingenuity, by its assistance, provided me the same evening with a very good loaf of bread. He had placed the iron pot on hot embers, having laid a large piece of tin, taken off one of the packages, over the mouth as a lid, and upon this he had strewed more embers. The loaf was supported in the middle of the vessel, between the two fires, upon cross sticks, and in this way a tolerably good oven was constructed.

The Canadians were now all busily employed in a work—that of erecting log-houses

—the simplicity and rapidity of which afforded an edifying lesson ; and the facility altogether of rearing a house from the ground to its summit appeared to be truly astonishing. To the Canadian labourer, accustomed to the use of the axe from his childhood, the felling of a tree is the act of a few minutes. He can drop it whichever way he pleases, divesting it of its limbs and adapting it for its place in the wall of the building with equal dexterity. Standing upon the fallen tree, and with his foot placed in such a position as would appear liable to be split to the instep at every blow, he strikes directly under it boldly and carelessly, thus making a large notch (which enters, perhaps, half the thickness of the tree) quite perpendicular. When the trees are all notched, nothing remains but to lay them in their places one upon another, or " the raising," as it is called. This done, the house is finished, and the tenant walks in,— happy if he has a door with a latch ready, and a window-frame with half a dozen panes of glass in it. Nothing then remains, but to plaster and calk with mud and moss *pro re natâ.*

By occasionally overlooking the men at work, and by working as hard as I could myself, I found the day pass quite agreeably, and was fatigued enough always before night. One of the huts in our knot was that of an officer, who commanded a detachment of Canadian fencibles; another, that of Captain P——, of the royal engineers; besides the Commodore's, with the red flag. But each of us had separate objects to employ his time; so that for a few days we saw very little indeed of each other. Captain C——, especially, was generally absent all day, employed in surveying the shores and taking the soundings of the bay.

March 3rd. — The weather, fortunately, was exceedingly fine, and the soft deep snow diminished sensibly under the influence of a brilliant sun. At the same time it was quite impossible to keep the feet dry, and I was wet through the whole of every day. This, however, did me no manner of harm; nor did I ever hear of any one of our party being otherwise than in perfect health, which was the more fortunate as we had no doctor among us. I have no doubt that the warmth kept up by the additional covering worn under the mocassins, which I have somewhere before described, was the means of counteracting the ill effects of the wet; and I believe that so long as the feet can be kept warm, no harm will ever ensue from damp: it is the cold which does the mischief. The most delicate subject is not afraid of a warm bath; he never complains of having been wet through, though he may have been half an hour in water up to the ears!

I worked all day with my axe, and had already let in a fine view of the bay, which was about a couple of hundred yards below me. My labour was repaid by every tree that fell; I improved in the use of the axe, and the whole aspect of things seemed more cheerful. Still I had no bed other than the spruce boughs which I strewed on my newly made bedstead ; so that there was good room for improvement, and a great deal to be done towards completing my little establishment.

March 4th.—The weather this day was much milder than usual, and the sun continued to shine all day.

March 5th.—A rapid thaw took place this day, attended with slight showers of rain. I was gratified by the appearance of a couple of crossbills, whose arrival I greeted as the harbingers of spring. The little creatures had probably flown a great way, being so tame from fatigue as to allow me to approach within three or four yards of them. The temperature was now really warm, and the weather seemed to be thoroughly breaking. Large ponds of clear water began to cover all parts of the bay, and the snow was so wet and slushy as to make walking intolerably bad ; at the same time it was so deep that it was difficult to make any progress without snow shoes. A pair hung up in my hut, but I had a horror of them ; and as I had no immediate object to induce me to visit distant

spots, I had waited till a change in the surface of the ground should render locomotion
more practicable. Now there was a prospect
of this. A hard frost would lay a crust upon
the snow, when I might walk as far as I
pleased : and this reflection was not a little
agreeable. In the mean time my log-house
was finished, and at a very little distance from
my hut ; but, as the weather was warm, I
grew so fastidious as to determine not to move
into it before it was well covered with shingles,
—a sort of covering for the sides and roof, of
the same kind, but more effectual than weather boarding. But, as there were no trees
quite fit for making these in the immediate
neighbourhood, I gave directions to one of the
men to go through the woods the next morning in order to find some that would answer the
purpose.—In the evening, much to my gratification, a sharp frost set in.

March 6th.—In the morning the aspect of
the country was altogether and totally changed. The snow was covered with a glassy
coating of ice, and the whole of the bay was

nearly frozen over. The pools of clear water
the day before had been so large and numerous, that an uninterrupted communication
from one to the other presented itself to the
eye ; and, as there had been no wind in the
night, the ice upon them was clear and good.
Instead of my mocassins, I put on a pair of
shoes, to which I had been for a long time
unused, and going down to the bay, sat down
upon a large stone to put on my skates. It
was a lovely morning ; the sun shone quite
bright, while the frost was remarkably keen ;
and in a very few minutes I was carried rapidly along towards the opposite shore. The
glow of exercise, the lively rattle of the skates,
and the sensation produced by the fresh air,
combined to embellish the novelty of the scene
before me, as I ranged with unlimited freedom
the clear ice which extended all across the bay.
Every object around me was unexplored, while
I had the means of being conveyed, as it were
on wings, from one to the other. I had been
confined for many weeks, either sitting still
half frozen in a carriage the whole of the day,

or, since my arrival in the forest, completely weather bound. For a long period I had never been thoroughly warm, only barely able to subdue cold, and had seldom during the whole day felt a dry stocking on my foot. My blood was now in full circulation, and the interest I felt in every thing around me was so great, that the sun had nearly reached the tops of the trees before I thought of returning to my dwelling. I had looked almost into every corner of the bay, which was about seven miles long and from two to three across, and was at last quite tired when I discovered an object which attracted my attention.

There was, at a distance on the ice, what appeared to be a mound of earth thrown up, —an appearance, under present circumstances, not to be readily accounted for; so I made towards it that I might see what it was. As I approached within a few hundred yards, I thought I perceived it move a little, and, halting for a moment, I saw that that was really the case. It was of a light-brown colour; but the figure was so indistinct, that while I watched it attentively I could not decide what it could possibly be. A bear would have been blacker, and I knew of no living creature of those regions answering its description. But, whatever it might be, there it was, and it was therefore necessary to be a little cautious, as I had no arms, in approaching it. I stood for some seconds thinking what I should do, and had almost determined to go home for my gun, when I saw the hide which caused all my speculation thrown suddenly aside to make way for the head and shoulders of an Indian, who protruded his rough matted locks into daylight from under it. This solved the problem in a moment, and I saw that the man had been employed in fishing, and had so completely enveloped himself in a large buffalo skin that no part of his body, head, feet, or hands, were to be discovered. He sat over a square hole cut in the ice, with a short spear ready to transfix any fish which might be attracted by his bait. The hole was about a foot square, and the bait was an artificial fish of white wood, with leaden eyes and tin fins, and about eight or nine inches long. The ice where he had cut it was about three feet thick.

Being within a few yards of him, I commenced a parley by signs, for he did not appear to understand a word of English; but he seemed to wish me anywhere else, and to be much annoyed at having been interrupted in his occupation. As my object was to pacify him, I gave him a small ball of twine I had in my pocket, and with this he was highly gratified ; much more so, however, by my skates, which he viewed with marks of great astonishment. He looked narrowly at the straps which bound them to my feet; but when I made him acquainted with their use, there were no bounds to his delight : at the same time he kept his own interest in view; for he tried to persuade me to give him a piece of a red shirt of flannel which I wore, to make a bait with. This I refused, by shaking my head and saying " No, no!" rather loudly; but he kept on entreating, taking hold of a corner of the collar with his finger and thumb.

I persisted in refusing, and kept him off. But he was not so easily answered, and offered me his knife, giving me to understand I might cut it from what part of the garment I pleased. So, shaking him by the hand and patting his shaggy locks, I skated away, leaving him to pursue his occupation for the rest of the evening.

On my return home I found that some cedar trees, fit for the purpose of making shingles, had been fixed upon in a part of the forest near the water's edge; that they had been felled, cut into lengths, and removed by means of small hand sleighs purposely prepared for them, and that the operation of splitting had already been commenced. These shingles are pieces of wood (as I may have already observed) resembling tiles, with which the roofs and sides of the better sort of houses are covered. As to houses, it may be generally remarked, that in these wild parts of the country, talking of a house, one composed simply of logs is understood, and if the idea of a more civilized dwelling is intended to be expressed, a frame house is the term made use of, which means one made with beams and rafters in the regular way. But to return to the shingles. They are by far better than weather boarding, in which, if a single nail by accident becomes displaced or loose, the evil extends itself more or less the whole length of the board, while the shingle, being less, fits close, and besides is not so liable to warp.

March 7th.—The frost continued, and the cold increased to a very low temperature, the effect of which, upon the extended sheet of ice which covered the bay, was somewhat re-markable. It cracked and split from one end to the other with a noise which might have been mistaken for distant artillery; but this, when it is taken into consideration that the sheet of ice was of fifteen or sixteen square miles area, and three feet thick, may be easily imagined. Nor was this all; I was occa-sionally surprised by sounds produced by the wind, indescribably awful and grand. Whe-ther the vast sheet of ice was made to vibrate

and bellow like the copper which generates
the thunder of the stage, or whether the air
rushing through its cracks and fissures produced the noise, I will not pretend to say;
still less to describe the various intonations
which in every direction struck upon the ear.
A dreary undulating sound wandered from
point to point, perplexing the mind to imagine
whence it came, or whither it went, whether
aerial or subterraneous; sometimes like low
moaning, and then swelling into a deep toned
note, as produced by some Æolian instrument:
it being, in real fact, and without metaphor,
the voice of winds imprisoned on the bosom of
the deep. This night I listened for the first
time to what was then perfectly new to me,
although I experienced its repetition on many
subsequent occasions, whenever the temperature fell very suddenly. The weather being
so excessively severe, I had added an extra
covering of spruce boughs to my hut, by
means of which, and the profusion of logs
which I heaped upon my fire, I was better
defended from its effects. Nevertheless, I

was obliged to rise before daylight, and heap
on eight or ten more, which lay ready for the
occasion, each of them as big as I could con-
veniently lift.

March 8th.—The air continued intensely
cold, so that, in spite of the sun, the most
violent exercise was necessary to preserve
warmth.   In the mean time my log house, a
palace compared to the hut I was in, was to
be ready before night, and the whole of the
day I felled trees, cut them into logs, hauling them in, and piling them up in my new
parlour; and the next morning I was to take
possession.   I lay down to rest on my spruce
boughs at night, satisfied with my day's work,
and pleased with my intended change of
dwelling.

March 9th.—I rose in the morning exhi-
larated by my projected movement, and the
weather at the same time seemed to smile
upon my operations; for the wind having
changed to another quarter, the warmth of
the sun so mellowed the air, that it was possible to stand still and look at surrounding

objects without feeling inconvenience from the cold. I got every thing ready, and my packages were soon tied together and distributed in separate burdens on the snow at the outside of my hut. My servant, with two or three of the Canadians, had arrived to carry them off, when an Indian, who carried a pair of snow shoes in his hand, as if he had just concluded a long journey, unexpectedly made his appearance. After some fidgeting, he produced an official letter, (from under his shirt,) which he had brought from York. The cover had been just strong enough for the service it had to perform, being worn through and through at every corner. I opened my letter and read my instructions to leave the establishment at Penetangushene, where I was, and return by the road I had come to Kempenfeldt Bay, and there await further orders. " Ibi omnis effusus labor." Not a green leaf then should I probably ever see on the banks of Lake Huron. My new dwelling and my avenues were to be abandoned. The wood I had piled with my own hands I

should never stay to burn, and all that remained was to make preparations for my immediate departure. The Indian had also
brought letters for Captain C—— and Captain P——, conveying similar instructions.
The whole establishment was to be broken
up, and all parties were to return nearer towards Quebec. On communicating together,
we all agreed to start at the same time the
next morning. The Canadians employed
themselves in making more hand sleighs for
the conveyance of the baggage of the party
over the ice, and as far as the state of the
snow, on the road through the forest, might
permit.

March 10th.—The morning broke with a
dry sparkling frost, and an hour after sun-
rise, the whole party was ready. The hand
sleighs were laden, each to be drawn by one
man, by means of a double trace crossing over
the breast. We bid adieu to the huts and
the log houses, and Captain C——, Lieut.
E——, and myself, together with the Canadians and shipwrights, all walked away over

the ice, the same way we had come towards the mouth of the bay. After walking some distance, I was enabled to skate for a few miles, and regretted I had not made the experiment sooner, for the ice then became so rough that it was impossible. The hand sleighs passed lightly over the hard surface, and the men who drew them were in the most jovial spirits. They whistled, sang, and ran races with each other along the ice, oversetting some of the sleighs, and breaking others, till a few miles' walk brought them to a more moderate tone of merriment. Such is the natural love of change, that we are made happy by it without knowing why or wherefore! But these men were doomed to receive before long a moral lesson, and lament the waste of strength, which they would have been wiser to reserve for the end of their walk. From the sleighs broken in these frolics, the loads had been transferred to others, and the delay occasioned by the accident was in each case made up by a hard run to catch the party, who went, not like a troop

P

of dragoons, according to the powers of the slowest horse, but on the contrary, every body entering into a quiet sort of determination within himself to walk away from his neighbour if he could. And thus, without giving or taking compliments, every body made the best of his way. And this was all very well, so long as the solid rough ice afforded a firm and not a slippery footing. However we came at last to the edge of the forest, where the road was altogether different. The surface of the snow was so exceedingly uneven, owing to the soft weather which had prevailed for some days before, that it was impossible to pull the hand sleighs along.

During the gambols of the English shipwrights, the Canadians had kept together, going all the while a steady pace; and now, for the first time, they and all the party halted. Libertè, a Canadian, a man in whose face the extremes of health and ugliness were combined, was the first at this juncture to prepare opposition to the dilemma. Libertè was evidently, in blood, half a savage; either by the father's or mother's side, he was the son of an Indian.   His constitution was strong as that of a bear.   Heedless of cold, a known and tried pedestrian, his short, thick figure betokened incalculable strength, and his swarthy features shewed a tinge too dark and fixed to be discomposed by common causes. He had suffered grievously from the small-pox, and he had only one eye, the other having been gouged * out about two years before by the thumb of a friend in a drunken squabble.   This man was in a moment on his knees unpacking the things in the sleighs and tying several of the bundles together, till he made a load as large as himself.   This, with the assistance of the other men, he placed on his shoulders, steadying it at the same time by a broad leathern belt which bore on his forehead.   Leaning his head backwards while the

* The American practice of " *gouging* " may not be generally known ; it is particularly simple, and very particularly cruel : a man twists his antagonist's hair firmly round his fingers, and having done so, takes the first opportunity afforded in the conflict, of poking out his eye with his thumb.

knot was fixing, as soon as all was ready, with the strength of a two year old bull, he darted it forward with a plunging effort, receiving thus nearly the whole of the weight upon his broad, thick neck; and then, at a strong shuffling trot, he had soon advanced many paces away from the party on his route through the forest. A very small portion of time was sufficient for the foregoing operation, and the rest of the Canadians, following the example of Libertè, were not less expeditious.

The English shipwrights, too, did the same with their baggage; but, being less accustomed to this mode of carrying burdens, they took necessarily some more time to make their arrangements. They made their handkerchiefs serve for the forehead strap, and contrived to divide the articles among themselves, so as to leave none behind; but notwithstanding, things were quite changed since the commencement of the journey. They grumbled and swore whenever one by accident ran against the other, making him trip or discomposing his load.   They were no longer the same boisterous crew, but whenever by accident their cords grew loose and required tightening, and they asked for assistance, it was in a civil, modulated tone that they addressed each other.   They strained hard to keep up with the Canadians, and, being all strong athletic fellows, were not left far behind, although they laboured grievously to maintain their place in the line of march.   At last it became absolutely necessary to keep the men together, for which purpose one of the Canadians was sent a-head to desire those in advance to moderate their pace ; for, unused as the English shipwrights were to a description of labour commonly adopted by the native Canadians in the country, it was soon evident that little progress would be made that day. And it was with great difficulty that, with the frequent delays to adjust the loads, and the very slow pace at best travelled, we were able altogether to reach the uninhabited hut where I had slept on my journey up, ten miles from Yeo river.   Our party took possession of this, while the Canadians and shipwrights repaired to another, which the former had made on their way to Penetangushene, and which was close by ours. It was impossible to sleep a great part of the night, owing to the noise they made. The men it appeared were carousing, and their loud peals of laughter were only interrupted by the songs which they, one after another, were called upon to sing. English and Canadians were unusually harmonious and friendly, and so we allowed them to follow their own devices, hoping that by and by a glance at their bundles might bring them to reason.

March 11th. We had twenty miles to go this day to Kempenfeldt Bay, and the travelling was not particularly bad. We were all ready at an early hour, although the shipwrights were far from lively. They argued about their loads, and the manner of securing them; for some of them were indeed very heavily laden. This was not all; for very few were quite sober. Those who were sober, were ill. One looked half asleep, another's eyes seemed starting out of his head; and all, it might fairly be said, were setting off under most unfavourable auspices. Nature seemed to be sinking within them, and they stopped to rest every quarter of an hour. Big drops of perspiration stood on the foreheads of those who lagged behind, while the foremost, heedless of every thing but themselves, left them to plod on alone. Thus, during the first two hours of the march, short as the journey was before us, it was by no means evident how long its accomplishment would take, owing to the large bundles, and the former evening's jollification. But by degrees the iron frames of these men overcame all their ailments; they rallied, and cheered up, till some of them joined in chorus with the Canadians, who sang as they travelled, so as to make the forest ring with the sound of their voices. We arrived at Kempenfeldt Bay in very good time. Captain C——, Lieut. E——, and myself, took possession of the log-house where I had slept on the night of the 26th of February, and the men were disposed of in another building of the same description, which had been erected close by for the purpose of depositing stores belonging to the navy. Lieut. E. was kind enough to lend me a hammock, of the use of which I availed myself with the more readiness as I had been sleeping every night in my clothes for a long time. The advantage, however, was purchased at some cost, for I had a severe fall, by which I not only cut my head, but demolished a good watch. The latter was at the time the most serious evil of the two.

March 12th to 14th. The weather during these three days was clear and cold; and as the bay was covered with good ice, I was enabled to skate over a considerable extent. All parties were waiting their instructions, and I felt in that state of uncertainty, as to be for the time rather indifferent to every thing. Letters were however received, which decided the fate of my companions. They were ordered to York, while a private communication gave me reason to expect that I should have to remain a considerable time where I was.

March 15th. At an early hour this morning, Captain C——, Lieut. E——, and the whole party of shipwrights, were ready for their journey to York, leaving me in the sole

possession of the log-house I was in.   I accompanied the party to the beach and a little
way over the ice, when, wishing them a good
journey, I returned back alone to my solitary
demesnes.   The fire had been neglected in
the bustle of departure, and had got low ;
remnants of packages and rubbish lay strewed
about ; my Canadians were at work at some
distance in the woods ; and there was nothing
to disturb the loneliness and silence of the place.
The building consisted of a single room of
sixteen feet by twelve.   The sides were rude
logs laid one upon another, and calked in so
insufficient a manner, that the light was visible
in more places than I was able to count.   The
door, of thin deal, was too ill fitted to fill
its frame, and the light which entered the
apartment was through a small window of
four panes of green inferior glass.—A gloomy
feeling invariably envelopes the mind, upon
finding one's self suddenly deserted, as it were,
and alone.   Without stopping to think why,
the very act of saying " good bye", and turning south while a friend or acquaintance walks
away to the north, is always sufficient to pro-

duce this in a slight degree, and at the instant I felt inclined to despond. But a remedy, the best of all others, immediately suggested itself, and I seized my axe, to receive, by a couple of hours' hard work in the woods, the benefit of my prescription.

Returning to my house through the snow, I found my servant had put every thing in order. The fire was replenished, and my simple repast was nearly ready. What was to be done? I had no books; and if I had, my house was too cold to sit still in. Reading, therefore, was out of the question. I fashioned a couple of forked boughs with my axe, to be fastened with a cord in a warm place over the fire, to support my gun, which I had taken out of its case, and put together; and, confiding in the private communication I had received, I resolved to fancy myself at least settled for some time to come in my present abode. The house of the Canadians was about 150 yards from mine; and with these men, my servant, whose services I seldom needed, resided. When I wanted his assistance, I opened my door, and shouted; and if the wind happened to set the right way, my summons was heard. If not, I was obliged to wade through the slushy snow, to fetch him. Rising soon after daylight, I immediately breakfasted; dined at noon, and supped at sunset. To prepare these meals cost little trouble; my toilette less; and the wood for my fire I chopped and piled myself; keeping the latter always alive both day and night. I began to make a bedstead, such as I had at Penetangushene, and spread moss and spruce boughs before the fire to dry, intending to make a bed whereon I could lie undressed, so soon as the bedstead was finished; for I had, besides my buffalo skin, four small blankets, as many sheets, and a strong rug. These arrangements took up nearly the whole of the day, and served to banish the apathy which, in the morning, had made me unwilling to attach myself to any sort of occupation.

March 16th. Before noon I had perfectly finished my bedstead, and heaped upon it as much spruce boughs and moss as necessary, confining the whole by a long cord made of strips of bark tied together, which I wound round and round till the whole was not only tight and compact, but soft withal to lie upon. This done, I laid my buffalo skin on the top, then my sheets and blankets—and all was ready. A large bundle of spruce boughs, confined with strips of bark, made also a good pillow. Having thus provided for my rest, I took my gun off the hooks over the fire, and sallied forth into the forest, in hopes of finding any thing to shoot, no matter what, that would come in my way. The snow had been frozen hard, but the top, thawed by the sun of the morning, was so soft, that sometimes I sank in up to my knees. The walking was excessively heavy and difficult, and the solitary appearance of the woods moderated my expectation of success. (I wore mocassins during my walk now, as at all other times, except when I was obliged to wear shoes for the purpose of skating.) The tracks of squirrels were abundant, and there were also some woodpeckers which I saw, speckled with white and scarlet; and I perceived on the snow the track of a larger bird, which, as it was quite fresh, I followed for a good way. It turned backwards and forwards and round and round, twisting about the trees in such a manner as to make it difficult to follow the track; and I was on the point of giving up the pursuit, when I heard the sound as of a pheasant rising into a tree close by me.   Turning round, I saw the partridge I had been pursuing, sitting on a bough, and shot him.   An unsportsmanlike act, certainly! but to be justified by the stupid disposition of the bird, which nothing can persuade to fly.   Besides, a pound of any sort of fresh meat was then to me a prize not by any means to be neglected. This was a beginning in the way of partridge shooting.   With game in the woods, there was an end of solitude; and so, blowing at the feathers of the bird, and minutely examining his plumage, I put him into my pocket, with the intention of having him, ere long, twirling at the end of a string before my fire. There are two sorts of these birds in this part of the country.   The birch partridge, such as the one I had just killed, and the spruce.   The former is the larger of the two, and the size of an English grouse. The bones are very slight, and the flesh white, and so extremely delicate as to render it impossible to carry it suspended by the head, as the body literally tears off by its own weight and the motion. The spruce partridge is a little smaller than the birch; the flesh much firmer and darker coloured, and bearing a strong flavour of the spruce fir. Both sorts perch on trees, and are fringed to the feet with feathers.

I pursued my walk, in the course of which I shot also a squirrel and a woodpecker, following the course of a ravine, at the bottom of which the snow lay in some places unusually deep; in others, more exposed to the sun, a stream might be detected gurgling through its deep, hollow channel, while the crackling surface, and the icicles which crowned the points of protruding rocks, bore evidence of the severe alternations of temperature. On the summit of the banks, in the warmest and most sheltered spots, the ground was already quite bare, and the green points of the early succulent plants were preparing to burst forth into their first leaves. The buds, too, on some of the trees, were distinctly visible. Thus, while the snow was distributed all over the woods in unequal proportion, so as to confine one's progress within small limits, the increasing power of the sun continued to diminish every day more and more the mass, giving additional strength to the consolatory hopes of approaching spring.

March 17th. This was a very tempestuous day. An unusually high wind hurried along clouds of small drifting snow, which penetrated the sides and roof of my house from top to bottom. Not a dry place was to be found in it; and upon my table, which stood close to the fire, I could write my name with my finger in the covering of snow which, like powder, lay upon it. The temperature, too, was exceedingly low. Finding it impossible to stay in the house, I took my axe and went to the most sheltered spot that I could find in the forest, where I worked, without stopping, till I made myself warm, when I returned home to dinner. The partridge had served me for supper the evening before, and now the squirrel and woodpecker were put before me in a pudding. The squirrel, being well peppered, tasted like a rabbit, and, I believe, was perfectly good. Something told me, however, that it was not right to eat the little animal, nor could I overcome my scruples. As to the woodpecker, I had no such compunction, nor was it necessary that I should. His flesh was his protection, being as black as that of an owl—absolute carrion! besides being lean and stringy. For that, however, I consoled myself. I was only a loser by the weight he carried on his bones, and that was so little, it did not much signify.

March 18th. This day I walked out again with my gun. I saw a flock of twenty or thirty birds about the size of fieldfares, or a little bigger, and somewhat resembling them in flight and action. They kept together on the tops of one tree after another, and on my pursuing them were very shy, and persisted in keeping out of distance. At the same time they were extremely noisy, and some of them were always chattering, while others whistled. I got near enough to see that their plumage was chiefly blue, and at last shot a straggler, as he flew over my head. I found he was a blue jay, a bird resembling the English jay in shape, and having also a similar black mark on the jaws.

New sounds and new colours now tended to enliven the solitary scene around me as each feathered stranger thus established his summer residence in the neighbourhood of my dwelling, ornamenting the forest with his brilliant plumage. It was beautiful to see the birds welcoming the budding leaf by their happy return from their long winter's banishment, while the eye followed their flitting track through the air, and the ear listened to notes lovely in themselves, and till then unheard.

March 19th. This day I went out shooting, but, owing to the violence of the wind, was actually obliged to return home. Indeed it was a service of danger to walk, for the dead branches were tumbling about my ears

Q

from the tops of the trees so frequently, that I had great difficulty to avoid them. The gale produced serious effects on every side. Some large decayed limbs fell, newly broken, to the ground, while others, long since severed and suspended among the boughs of their neighbours, now loosened their hold. The crash of trees falling around was so frequent as to be to me really astonishing. Indeed, in calmer days I had often reflected on the subject. Even in the finest weather, hardly a quarter of an hour ever passes in a North American forest, when, if one listens, a tree is not heard to fall to the ground; so often, as, apparently, ill to accord with the extended duration of vegetative life. But the discrepancy is reconciled by drawing an analogy with human existence. Sometimes the sweeping hurricane, like a virulent disorder of our race, levels the tenants of the forest prematurely with the earth;—but Time ever stalks abroad, closing days and centuries. And if, in the dense assemblage of the woods, where such unnumbered multitudes exist, these instances of universal mortality should be at all times occurring, the summons, with reference to the numbers within hearing, is no more to be wondered at, than that the village bell should daily toll, unregarded, the knell of more short-lived man. *** Having returned home to my house, such as it was, I had scarcely arrived when a snow storm set in, which lasted the whole of the day. I had but little occasion for a candle in the evening: if I had, it would not have been possible to keep one burning. My blazing, companionable fire afforded light for all my present purposes, and I heaped on it a pile of maple logs sufficient to set the tempest at defiance; for winter seemed to have recommenced in all its rigours.

March 20th. Very early this morning I was awakened by a scratching at my door; and on listening attentively, I distinctly heard the feet of some animal which evidently had an intention of making its way into the house. It put its nose to the bottom of the door, snuffling and whining from eagerness, after the manner, as I thought, of a dog. Con-

ceiving it might possibly be either a bear or a
wolf, without stopping to put on my clothes,
I seized my gun, which was ready loaded over
the fire, and keeping my eyes upon the door,
which was of such very thin deal, and so imperfectly fastened by a wooden latch, that I
could place no confidence whatever in its
strength, I remained still a moment or two,
not making up my mind exactly what to do.
My window was fixed, and the glass so bad,
that light would barely pass through it. As
to distinguishing any object on the other side,
that was quite impossible. There was many a
hole in the house of which I might have availed
myself, but it was scarcely daybreak, and
therefore too dark to discern any thing without.
So I threw a small log or two upon the fire to
blaze up, thinking it best to remain where I
was, even in case the creature should happen
to break into the house, when I should be sure
to have a fair shot at it. Scarcely a minute
had now elapsed from the very beginning,
when I concluded, from the sound, the perseverance, and total absence of fear of the animal, that it must be a dog, and nothing else;

so I opened the door very little and with extreme caution, and discovered, to my surprise and satisfaction, that I was right; for a dog it was; and in an instant, a brown, rough water-spaniel bounced into my room, overjoyed at having reached a human habitation. To account at once for the circumstance:—My house was but little removed out of the line of march of the North-west traders; to one of which persons (as I afterwards discovered) the dog had belonged; and having lost his master, had wandered through the forest, till he came by chance to my dwelling.

I greeted him with a most cordial welcome, happy to have a companion! an honest friend! whether from the clouds or elsewhere, no matter: so wishing his former master, whoever he might be, all sorts of worldly prosperity, my only hope was, that he might never shew his face in my neighbourhood; and I put a string round the neck of the dog. The poor fellow was, on his part, just as happy to see me as a dog could well be. He frisked and jumped, wagging his tail, and licking my hands, while his eloquent eyes, as plainly as letters engraved on brass, besought me to make trial of the merits of one so ready, on his part, to execute a bond of faithful allegiance. I shewed him my gun, holding it down low to his nose; upon which he held his head back, while a glance of recognition ratified the treaty. Calling immediately for my servant, I got my breakfast; not forgetting my new guest. I had nothing for myself but bread and salt pork, which I shared with him. He ate voraciously, having been, apparently, a long time without food. I tried all the names of dogs, in order to see to which he answered best; and at last fancied that he attended most to that of Rover. So Rover, at all events, I determined to call him.

To sportsmen, at least, it may be readily imagined that no time was expended in useless preparation, before we sallied forth together, without farther ceremony, in quest of game, into the forest. The snow in the woods was crisp from the night's frost; the sun was just rising in a clear sky. I, that yesterday had no resource but to track a poor unfortunate bird by its footsteps, had now my gun on my shoulder, my dog before me, and the best of a fine day unexpended. The haunts of a description of game, of which I was totally ignorant, were evidently familiar to my dog; and as he quartered his ground from right to left, I felt the most eager interest and curiosity in the pursuit. I had walked about half an hour, when he suddenly quested; and on going up to him, I found him at the edge of a swamp, among a clump of white cedar trees, on one of which he had evidently treed some description of bird; for he was looking stedfastly up into the tree, and barking with the utmost eagerness. I looked attentively, but nothing whatever could I discover. I walked round the tree, and round again, then observed the dog, whose eyes were evidently directly fixed upon the object itself, and still was disappointed by perceiving nothing. In the mean time, the dog, working himself up to a pitch of impatience and violence, tore with his paws the trunk of the tree, and bit the rotten sticks and bark, jumping and springing up at intervals towards the game; and five minutes had at least elapsed in this manner, when all at once I saw the eye of the bird. There he sat, or rather stood, just where Rover pointed, in an attitude so perfectly still and fixed, with an outstretched neck and a body drawn out to so unnatural a length, that twenty times must I have overlooked him, mistaking him for a dead branch, which he most closely resembled. He was about twenty feet from the ground, on a bough, and sat eight or ten feet from the body of the tree. So, retreating to a little distance, I shot him. This done, I pursued my way, and in the course of the morning killed four more partridges, which I came upon much in the same way as I did upon the first. My larder was now handsomely stocked with game. The snow became as usual very soft in the middle of the day, so that I never was otherwise than quite wet through about the feet and legs. To have a house of my own, however, and the advantage of an excellent fire, by far more than compensated for other inconveniences, and I felt a growing interest in every thing about me.

March 21st.—During the whole of this day the weather was particularly mild, but the hard night frosts continued to preserve the vast quantities of snow, with which the ground and the ice in the bay was covered. I went out again with my dog for a few hours in the morning, and brought in some more partridges. At one of these my gun flashed three times without his attempting to move, after which I drew the charge, loaded again, and killed him. The dog all the time was barking and baying him with great perseverance. There is no limit to the stupidity of these creatures, and it is by no means unusual on finding a whole covey on a tree in the autumn, to begin by shooting the bird which happens to sit lowest, and then to drop the one above him, and so on till all are killed; and this has very often been done.

March 22d.—The Canadians had been for the last few days employed in making a landing place or wharf for boats of pine logs, and they had been put to some inconvenience from the want of a file to set a large cross cut saw; so I had dispatched Libertè across the lake, to Newmarket, in order to purchase half a dozen at Mr. Peter Robinson's shop. It was a long way to send for a few files, (forty-seven miles thither, and forty-seven back, in such weather,) particularly as the snow on the bay was so very deep and slushy that nobody but such a being as Libertè would have gone across, the danger of breaking into holes at this season of the year being very great. However, this day, back he came, having made the journey in a very short time, though I do not recollect the precise number of hours he was on his way. Libertè gave me the files, and at the same time produced a large piece of the flesh of a bear which some Indians, whom he had met on the way, had given to him. It was a great lump of black looking meat, very much like horse-flesh, without the least particle of fat about it; however, as I knew it was usually eaten in the country, notwithstanding the appearance, I felt not the least objection to make an experiment upon it, and I had it for dinner the same day. But there was something so very disagreeable in the taste, so extremely fusty, as if it had been kept in a close cupboard, or a hot pocket, that with all my inclination to dine on fresh meat, I could not eat an ounce of it. Nor could my servant touch it. But Rover had no scruples of any sort, and ate the whole.

March 23d to April 2d.—The weather was very mild during the whole of this period, although the frosts at night were regular and severe. There seemed to be really no end to the snow, which was however, on the whole, decreasing. I contrived with my gun and my axe to employ my time, and to set ennui and blue devils at defiance. I commenced preparations for the coming of the wild fowl, of which I heard exaggerated histories from the Canadians; and in the sequestered spots at the edge of the bay, I cleared away trees to let in a sufficient view of the water, and, with the branches, I made ambuscades in those places most likely for their resort. And this was an object in which I was so much interested, that it took much time and labour to carry it into execution. But I worked hard and regularly in order to have my operations finished before the breaking up of the ice in the bay, which event I expected to take place in about ten days, and then, as I heard, the wild fowl would come pouring in in great numbers. I had already seen a great many flights of both ducks and geese, but all so remarkably high in the air, as to make it evident they were bending their course to some point very remote.

April 3d.—The day was dark and cloudy. Alternate showers of snow and sleet penetrated the sides of my house, which was nearly as full of holes as a sieve. A little rain fell towards the evening, and the general unsettled appearance of the weather held out reasonable expectations of a speedy break up of the frost.

April 4th.—Shortly after daylight, in the morning, I heard a chattering of birds close

to my house, as loud and incessant as if a
thousand parrots had perched upon the neigh-
bouring trees.   I hurried on my clothes, and
taking my gun in my hand, was out of doors
in the space of two or three minutes.   The
day was unusually soft and mild, and there
was a fog so dense that I could only see a
few yards before me.   It was quite spring
weather, and the snow was thawing as fast as
it possibly could.   I soon perceived that a
flock of wood pigeons had settled themselves
all round about me, though I was surprised
at the note so little resembling that of any
sort of pigeon I had ever heard.   Indeed I
can think of no better comparison than the
one already chosen.   As I approached towards the busy gabbling which directed my
course, the first that struck my eye had perched on the branches of a dead old tree, which
was literally laden with them.   They stuck
all over it as thick as they could possibly sit.   I
had no sooner caught sight of them than they
immediately rose, and this movement was the
signal for legions of others, which I could not

see, to do the same. It was unlucky that the fog was so thick, or the sight must have been grand; there seemed to have been enough to have carried me away with them, house and all. I shot at them as they rose, but I was rather too late, and only killed four. However, I had no sooner loaded my gun, when I found that some of the stragglers were flying about in circles, and settling themselves in the different trees. I therefore continued the pursuit, and before breakfast I had bagged in all twenty-two birds. This description of wood pigeon which visits the country in such prodigious flocks, is about the size of the English dove-house pigeon; the bill is however longer, and the form of the body more tapering and slender. On the wing, their shape and flight exactly resemble that of a hawk; like him, they twist and turn among the branches of the trees with astonishing strength and rapidity. The tail also, like that of a hawk, is long; and their colour is blue. Towards the middle of the day, the sun broke out through the fog, and it became hot. The

ice in the bay, covered over with watery
slushy snow, now began to put on an appearance of breaking up totally. It had melted
away entirely round the edges, and in some
places, twenty yards or more of clear water
intervened between it and the shore.

April 5th.—A sudden change in the weather took place, and it became much colder,
with frost. This day I received a communication from York, by which I understood that
I might for some time consider myself settled
where I was, and of this I was by no means
sorry,—many a worse situation might have
been devised for me. Some of my Canadians
were to be dismissed, and the man who brought
my letter had orders to remain and to place
himself at my disposal. This man had been
accompanied over the ice, which was now unsound and extremely dangerous, by a respect-
able Scotchman, a Mr. F——, who brought
with him his wife and a young child. Mr.
F—— had been persuaded to proceed thus
far on a speculation, founded on the hopes of
a military establishment being to be formed

on the banks of Lake Huron, where he had
intended to commence business as a pub-
lican, but he had no sooner arrived than he
discovered, that whether owing to having listened to bad advice, or otherwise, he had
already, " in taking the Red Cow, made a
devil of a bull." He appeared a sober, industrious man, and I really pitied his forlorn prospects; for he had been induced to leave a
more eligible spot, and had now gone too far
to recede. He commenced felling trees for
his log house instantèr, in the mean time taking up his abode in the house with the Canadians. Those who were to depart had already gone off in high spirits, at a time when,
certainly, although the frost had temporarily
improved the state of the ice, a heavy gale
of wind, had it chanced to set in, must have
broken up every atom of it, and have drowned
the whole party.

April 6th.—A tempestuous day with showers of sleet, towards the evening rather warmer, but still windy. Mr. F——, in despite of
the weather, persevered at his labour. He

was a strong, able fellow, and the precision with which the long slashing cuts of his axe followed each other in the same identical line, was extraordinary to look at.

April 7th.—A cold and rainy day.

April 8th.—The weather again warm and foggy.

April 9th and 10th.—Cold windy weather.

April 11th.—Large cracks now began to appear in the ice, traversing across and the whole length of the bay. By its extreme thickness it nevertheless held together most obstinately. Nearly the whole surface was covered with water. It was now perfectly impassable. I killed a bird about the size of a jackdaw, and very like one, except that he was only grey close round the eyes. I also shot a woodpecker, about as large as a dove, with a black mark on the jaws and a bright scarlet spot on the pole. Large patches of ground, quite clear of snow, now appeared in the woods in those places the most exposed to the sun.

R

I discovered a quantity of wild leeks just shooting up out of the earth, of which I gathered a good many. I was unfortunate in this, my first essay on vegetable diet, for they heated me to such a degree, that I was for some time afraid they had possessed some deleterious quality; but the intolerably high flavour of the plant quieted my apprehensions. I was in a burning fever, at the same time quite sure that I had eaten nothing but leeks. Though they abounded all over the woods, for a long time afterwards I was too well satisfied with my first dose ever to try another. I shot some partridges, also a striped squirrel, a harmless little creature, somewhat less than the English squirrel.

April 12th.—The length of the days being considerably increased, the forest assumed every hour a more vernal appearance. Still none but the earliest trees, and those only in the warmest situations, were in forward bud. As yet, unrelentless winter had not loosened the ice, which bound up the waters in the bay, and every night destroyed the hopes that each morning had created of an event now most wofully protracted.

I had walked this morning, with my gun on my shoulder, some distance from my house, considerably farther than I had ever ventured before, having come upon a spot so clear from snow, as to induce me to extend my ramble, as the day was fine, without thinking of my return. Trusting only to my footsteps, and neglecting all other means of precaution, it was not till I began to attempt to return home, that I perceived I was bewildered and unable to find my way back. I grew very eager, and ran backwards and forwards in the hopes of being able to retrace the path by which I had arrived at the spot where I was, but to no purpose : at last I came quite to a stand still, and very soon became completely puzzled. Very uncomfortable reflections immediately suggested themselves, not at all calculated to assist the dilemma, and they were not much relieved when, having climbed to the top of a high tree, I could see nothing but the waving

summits of trees in all directions. I began
to think of my own folly, and the change in
my life and prospects thus effected within the
space of a few short minutes. I might, by
good fortune, find my way back, but should I
take a wrong course, the long odds were certainly against me. Not to make a bad matter
worse, I thought it as well to sit still and
think a little, being moreover as near the
summit of the tree as I could venture, without
the immediate chance of breaking my neck.
Having observed the highest spot of ground,
and taking the best observation I could of the
direction of this point, I descended and made
towards it, notching the branches as I went
on with my knife. Then making choice of
the highest of the trees, I climbed to the top,
where I received payment in full and com-
pound interest for my trouble, by catching a
glimpse of the ice in the bay. I very joyfully
made towards it, marking the trees in my way
as before, and having arrived at the shore,
found I was not more than three miles from
my house, to which I bent my steps as straight

as possible; so much so as to toil pretty hard in clambering over the trunks of the huge trees which impeded my progress, and floundering through the deep snow.

My exertions brought to my mind reflections relating to the scanty way I had provided myself with clothes, for I had not calculated upon the extra wear and tear to which my manner of life subjected my wardrobe. What with working with my axe, moving and piling heavy logs, and such sort of occupations, I had been for some days past very much out at elbows; and when I got home, after this morning's adventure, the state of my dress was a matter of serious consideration. In climbing the trees, I had really left parts of my things sticking on the branches, from the eagerness with which I went up and down, and now that I came to take a cool survey of myself, I found that I was literally in rags, and that too without a tailor to help me. I had, however, needles and thread in abundance, which nothing but sheer necessity could induce me to use; but the time was come, and I employed myself upwards of two hours in the evening, by the light of the fire, in cutting out patches, and sewing them on as well as I could.

April 13th.—I shot one of the large sort of woodpeckers, called by the Canadians " cocks of the wood ", in size rather larger than a carrier pigeon, with a bright scarlet crest. The Indians apply the scarlet feathers of this bird to many articles of ornament. This day I was very near losing my servant, who had been amusing himself, during my absence from home in the morning, by standing upon the large slabs of ice, which, having broken off from the main body, were floating at the edge of the bay. And he ferried himself about, as on a raft, with a long pole ; but the piece he was upon split in the middle, and he had a hard struggle for his life, being perfectly unable to swim, and away from all manner of assistance. He was severely bruised, and drank more water than was of service to him, so that he was very ill the rest of the day.

April 14th.—I had it in contemplation some days past, to make my way through the forest to the head of the Notawasorga river, on objects connected with the duty on which I was engaged; and as the weather seemed to-day to favour the expedition, I applied to the Canadian, Libertè, to accompany me thither as a guide. I have already described the land communication from Kempenfeldt Bay, through the forest, to Lake Huron. Another road had, however, been cut, by which the land journey was considerably shortened, but it was in a rude state, being merely a track where the trees had been partially felled by the axe, and the stumps even of these very imperfectly removed. This road led from the end of Kempenfeldt Bay, straight to the Notawasorga river, making a portage of eight miles. Thence stores of all descriptions were in the season to be transported in batteaux, or flat bottomed boats, down the river (a narrow sedgy stream) to Lake Huron, and put on board the government schooners appointed for their conveyance across the lake to the upper port of Michilimackinac. Thus the line of transport all the way from York was, from thence by land to Holland River, communicating with Lake Simcoe. From Holland River, by water, to the head of Kempenfeldt Bay, an outlet of Lake Simcoe. By land, across the portage of eight miles, to the Notawasorga River, and thence by water to Lake Huron. The log house in which I was living, was about three miles from the head of the bay, to which point no road had yet been cut, and I started with Libertè, first keeping along the shore of the bay till we reached the track, and then pursuing it to the head of the Notawasorga River.

Libertè possessed, in common with the Indians, the faculty of crossing the woods to any point he wished, and proposed to make a straight line in this instance, instead of keeping along shore; but I had but recently experienced the sensation of being lost, and I had no wish to run any unnecessary risk. The distance we had to go and return was only twenty-two miles, and the Canadian, whatever his confidence in himself might have been, had neither ideas nor words to make me at first feel sure enough of his skill to

trust him. When he talked of the rough sides
of the trees as the appearance by which he
determined his bearing, I could not but remark, that to my view the rough sides of the
trees seemed to point half round the compass,
and to this objection, urge it how I would, he
could say nothing explanatory or convincing.
However, during our walk along the track,
he related to me so many journeys he had
undertaken by himself in this way, that my
curiosity predominated, and I determined to
allow him, on our return, to strike at once
homewards through the forest.   Although he
had not the means of communicating his faculty of finding his road, so as to make himself at all intelligible, he spoke very reason-
ably on the subject of another talent, known
to be possessed in a great degree by the native Indians; that of tracking a man or any
animal over all sorts of ground and among
dry leaves.   And this he was able to account
for (to my mind) very satisfactorily as follows.   The forests in North America are generally without brambles or underwood, the
soil being little more than rotten wood, a com-

post which takes the impression of a foot like dough. It is different in England, for there the little fibrous roots, creeping through the soil, interlace each other, and form as it were a springy frame-work rising up under the foot of a man, or even of a horse, without leaving any impression. The trunks of trees also, which lie about in such profusion, and are chiefly covered thickly with moss, most materially assist the pursuit, for no animal can proceed without passing over them, and leaving vestiges of its progress by rubbing off the moss.

We walked a good pace till we reached the point of our destination, and having remained there a short time, so as to satisfy myself as to the objects I had in view, we commenced our return; and leaving the track, plunged at once into the recesses of the forest, and were immediately out of sight of the road altogether. Libertè was now in his proper element, and though I followed him as fast as I could, I was often obliged to call out to desire him to moderate his pace. The ground was very unequally covered with snow. In most places it was quite bare, in some we were obliged to wade above our knees, and in particular parts where it had drifted, we were driven out of our line in order to go round. The huge trees which, after flourishing for ages, had been blown down in their decline by the high winds, crossed our path with such frequency, that the operation of climbing was repeated as often as during a walk through a country enclosed by stone walls in England. But a large tree is not so easily passed as a wall, the passage over it being generally only practicable where the trunk is of large dimensions. And a traveller has no choice, for the roots and branches extend too far on each side to make it worth while to go round, even when they do not come in contact with those of other fallen trees; and several of these frequently lie extended in the same direction. Libertè, from long practice, vaulted over them with great ease and alacrity, and I, with more difficulty, followed him as well and as fast as I could. But it was impossible to avoid stopping every

now and then to observe the stupendous bulk
of some of the trees, the great age of which
had rendered them most truly objects of admiration. The magnificent outline of some
of these, and the tranquil gloom of the forest
altogether, was indescribably impressive and
grand.

In these wild haunts, neglected, though
subservient to the purposes of man, nature
seemed to have held for ages her undisturbed
reign. Where I stood, perhaps the foot of a
civilized being had never before trodden. I
contemplated a vegetative world, following in
regions of unlimited space, the laws of creation
to maturity, and then sinking in every stage
of natural decay, till all mingled again with
its parent earth. Here, a tree lay prostrate
on the ground perfect in its form and covered
with thick moss. Attempt but to pass it and
the feet sink deep in rotten wood, while the
strength of an infant's arm might scatter its
vast yielding bulk in dust over the land.
There what *was* a giant pine, now a low
green mound, sunken by gentle degrees to the

very level of the earth, recalled to the mind
the time, when after a few more short years,
all remaining traces of its existence should be
obliterated, till like those which in preceding
ages had passed away, it should become confounded together and mixed with the soil.

The varying duration of animal life, the return of seasons, the orbits of the planets, even
the eccentric course of comets become defined,
and familiarized with our ideas of time, by
the inquiring spirit and science of man; but
the tree still rears its head towards the heavens in defiance of his research, while tradi-
tion and conjecture alone mark the span of its
existence.   Generations after generations of
the human race have fallen one after another
into the grave, and yet in this enlightened age
where is the man who can count the years of
the gnarled oak?   Can he mark the day when
it burst its acorn with much more certainty
than he could define the period when each
stream and river first bubbled from the ca-
verns of the earth?   How grand is the de-
sign of nature presented to the view in these

profound forests of North America! A continent abounding in images, not only calculated to magnify the ideas of time and space, but to exalt in the imagination the Creative power, whose wise ordinances thus hold in preparation so vast a field for the unborn millions destined at some future (perhaps not distant) day to inhabit a country, commensurate in its gigantic features with the ever expanding powers of modern improvement.

The Canadian continued his line with determined precision, and without adopting any visible means of precaution, till we arrived at spots in the neighbourhood of my log-house, which I had visited before and were known to me. We were about an hour's walk from home when we came to a wigwam, where an old Indian and his squaw were roasting part of the flesh of a porcupine before the embers of a fire. The meat was transfixed by a straight stick, and thrust down within a little of one of its ends, which rested on the ground, while the squaw sat away from the fire and turned it round by the other. I was anxious

to try a morsel, which was readily given to
me, but it tasted so much of smoke, that I
could perceive no other taste in it; besides,
it looked very bad indeed. I observed the
way the Indian had made his fire. He had
rested the ends of three or four logs, of about
six feet long, upon two very short ones, placed
across and parallel to each other, and then set
fire to the long ones in the middle. So soon
as they were burnt through, he continued to
keep the lighted ends together till the whole
were consumed, replacing them with fresh
ones. The old Indian was extremely perse-
vering in his demands for something to drink,
and I had nothing to give him but a dollar,
which he looked at with much discontent. I
had no less coin, and it was more than would
have been necessary, under other circumstances, to have contented him; but to these
people, the present hour is every thing; and
one single glass of liquor, to be then and there
received, would have purchased the post-obit
of a much larger quantity.

April 15th.—This morning the weather

appeared to have changed altogether. The ground was covered with snow which lay about four inches deep. The sun, however, came out with considerable force, and it was melted and had thoroughly disappeared before one o'clock. The ice in the bay still held together, although nearly covered with water. I shot a bird, called by the natives a robin, being the size of a blackbird, and in colour like the redwing, with a yellow bill.

April 16th.—The weather cloudy but warm. On going out this morning I met with several small green snakes, which were perfectly harmless. There is not, I believe, any sort of noxious reptile in this part of the country. The snakes rapidly increased to such numbers, that in a very few days it was perfectly impossible to pursue a morning's walk without treading on one or more of them. Where the sun shone warm, they were sometimes to be met with as numerous as earth worms in England, after a shower of rain.

April 17th.—A strong wind having set in in the night, blowing directly out of the bay,

I perceived in the morning all the ice broken in pieces, and floating towards the lake. It was moving slowly away, and a considerable extent of water was already uncovered. This was a joyful sight, for of all things a sheet of water conveys the most lively impressions to the mind, and confined as I was from the impassable state of the ice to the shores on one side of the bay, the barrier was no sooner removed than I felt a sensation of liberation, which seemed to be participated by the turbulent waves themselves, as, just risen from their bondage, they rallied as it were and held council together, bubbling and fretting in their eagerness to press on the rear of their retiring enemy. The wind chased the chilly field before it, which, split into mammocks, was every minute retiring farther from the sight, till about three o'clock in the afternoon, when the lively change was altogether perfect, and Kempenfeldt Bay, so long the type of dreary winter, became a lovely basin of pure water. And, as if to add to the gratifying occurrence, the ice had no sooner disappeared,

s

than the wind lulled, and the sun beamed forth
to embellish the natural beauties of a spot in
themselves very much above the common
order. As the evening advanced, it was beautiful to see the enormous pines with which the
banks were fringed, reflected in the water,
while the winding shore presented a pleasing
variety of sandy beach and bluff, rocky headland. Nor were the animal creation insensible
to the moment: the large fish leaped incessantly
high out of the water, and it was scarcely
dark before a flock of wild fowl flew round
and round in circles, lowering themselves by
degrees, till each, one after another, dashed
heavily into the favourite element. A sports-
man can readily comprehend how animating
it was to listen to the wild sounds which now
broke upon the ear, as the feathered troop held
their gabbling conversation together, and diving and splashing by turns, they commenced
every now and then a short flight for the sake of
a fresh launch upon the water. Every thing
now was new; Nature had thrown off her
homely winter's garb, and was beginning to

unveil her beauties. My enjoyments were from that day increased, and fish and fowl were added to my resources.

It seemed wonderful to think there should be so few among our poorer classes with energy enough to break the chains of poverty, and visit a land where pauperism is yet unknown; where youth and strength supply the catalogue of human wants, and where industry must meet its sure reward. The exuberant abundance of wood for fuel renders the fire-side of the peasant, during the long evenings of winter, a solace equal to that of many a wealthier citizen of the world, and as his children, with united strength, drag in each log to the hearth, he rejoices in the clearance of the encumbered earth, when those of the civilized world pay dearly for the enjoyment of warmth. An emulative feeling stimulates the natural industry of his constitution. The rattling clank of a neighbour's axe, the crashing fall of a heavy tree, seem to demand responsive exertion on his part, and give rise to an energy, which, even if the tinkling frosty air at his fingers' ends fails to re-

s 2

mind him that he has work on hand, quickly rouses within him the spirit of active labour. The work of his young children is of a value to him, far exceeding the expense of their maintenance, and he lives in the enjoyment of the consciousness of being able to leave them an inheritance of peace, if not of affluence. With facilities of water carriage, fish in abundance, and fuel, by the help of his gun, he may complete the necessaries of life, and while the partridge and wild pigeon supply him with variety in food, he has also in store both recreation and amusement. It was long after dark when I returned to my house from the banks of the bay, and the night had far advanced before the various sounds of the different descriptions of wild fowl had ceased, as they settled themselves in their new domain.

April 18th.—I had made preparation for the wild fowl, by forming ambuscades in several places on the borders of the bay; and to one of these I made my way this morning an hour before daylight. The wild fowl kept themselves in the middle of the bay, but I shot a large sort of kingfisher, slate-coloured, with a black crest, and as large as a pigeon. In going home, I saw the head of a small animal, which I thought was a pole-cat, protruded from a hole in an old tree. I took a stick from the ground and killed it, when, to my mortification, I found it was a flying squirrel with four young ones.

The snow might now be said to be entirely dissipated in the woods, excepting in the ravines and places where the drift was extraordinarily deep.

I was aroused in the night by the yelping of a wolf out of doors, close by my house. As I listened, I heard the sound again farther off, and so on till he went quite away. He had no doubt received intelligence of the breaking up of the ice, and had come to meet with his prey on the shores of the bay. My dog was in the room, but took no notice of the noise, which he must have heard.

April 19th. I was up again before daylight, and with better success. I killed nine wild fowl of different sorts before breakfast,

not one of which could I eat, the flesh being
so black and fishy.

I saw a canoe paddled by a couple of Indians
advancing slowly along shore, and I hailed
them, but they were at first unwilling to attend
to me, although I succeeded at last in bringing
them to a parley; and found they had two or
three large fish in the bottom of their canoe.
I made signs that if they would come a little
way with me I would give them something to
drink, and that I wanted to buy the fish. One
of them, a very old man, appeared to assent to
my proposal, and, taking the fish by the gills,
accompanied me to my house.   In my way
thither I called at the Canadian's house for Libertè, who spoke the Indian language as well
as his own.   I was very soon owner of a large
salmon; and after proper time had elapsed, (for
a bargain takes time all over the world,) and
not before the eyes of the Indian began to roll
in his head from the liquor I had given him
to drink, he agreed to terms for some other
articles I proposed to purchase. And I bought
of him the canoe, which he had left with his

friend at the water's edge, and a fish-spear.
For the fish-spear, the fish, and the canoe, I
paid him nine dollars, which was quite as much
as the things were worth. When we returned
to the canoe, the friend seemed to have no objection to the bargain; but as I saw that the
happy state of the old man was all he envied,
I gave him drink enough to make him equally
stupid; and then, tying up the old man's nine
dollars tight in the bosom of his coat, left both
to complete their adventures in each other's
company, and I never saw them any more.

I was now ready to go out the first calm
evening and spear fish with Libertè, who told
me he understood the art perfectly well. The
present day, however, would not answer the
purpose; for the slightest possible ripple on
the water makes it impossible to see the fish
under the surface. Libertè undertook to collect the bark of the birch tree in sufficient
quantity for our expedition, whenever the weather should turn out perfectly favourable, and
examined the canoe, to see that nothing was
wanting.

April 20th. I breakfasted very early on

the remainder of my fish, which had been cut into large pieces and broiled on the embers. It was a large sort of salmon-trout, but neither firm nor high-flavoured. Under circumstances, it was most thankfully received for better. I went out in quest of wild fowl, and shot several; among them a species of black duck. The wild fowl, generally, were much more fishy than in England, with the exception of this latter species. I saw a troop of saw-bill divers, which had taken possession of a small inlet close to the shore, where their pyebald colour and pert crests looked most inviting. Some craggy land overhung their position, which I gained unperceived, when they were all below me in a lump; twelve, or upwards, within thirty yards, and in deep water. On my firing, they disappeared like witchcraft. Not one was hit; and they were so long under water, that I could hardly recognize the flock when they re-appeared at a great distance. In my hurry to load again, I found I had lost my powder-horn; to me then a very serious misfortune. I had no means of replacing it, otherwise than by the wretched substitute of a small bag, which I made of squirrel skins, and a measure cut out of a piece of wood.

April 21st. The evening turned out remarkably fine, and the water was as smooth as a looking-glass. Every thing was ready for my fish-spearing expedition, the preparations for which were extremely simple. The fish-spear consisted of a straight handle about fifteen feet long, to which a couple of barbed iron spikes, of sufficient size to pierce a moderate-sized salmon, were affixed. The birch-bark, for the purpose of light, was prepared in pieces three or four double, each the size of a large quarto book; and one at a time of these was stuck in a cleft pole five or six feet long, placed at the head of the canoe, overhanging the water in such a manner that the blazing bark might shine upon it. It was no sooner dark than I went to the water's edge, where Libertè and another Canadian were ready with the canoe. As he held the vessel to the shore I steadied myself by his shoulder, stepped in cautiously, and took my seat in the middle. The canoe

was a very egg-shell, and as cranky as a wash-
ing-tub, more fitted to carry ghosts than men,
while Libertè was as ugly as Charon himself.
A boy of twelve years old could have carried
it, notwithstanding it was to hold three of us.
We had an establishment of tinder and matches,
and some pieces of fat pork cut into slips as a
substitute for candles.

As soon as we embarked, the men paddled
away along shore towards the head of the bay;
and as soon as we came near some small
streams which set into the bay, we stopped,
and the men, having struck a light, kindled the
birch-bark in the cleft pole. Crackling like
soft fat, the unctuous matter produced a clear
flame, which lighted up the watery depth be-
neath us to the brightness of day. The soft
ashes which fell occasionally from the fire
caused a ripple, which for a moment confused
the objects underneath, but otherwise at a
depth of ten feet every thing was clear and
resplendent. The slightest form was distinctly visible,—every pebble, even the beetle
that crawled on the ground. We passed

some perch lying close to the bottom, and
soon afterwards a rapid quiver of the water
announced the presence of some larger fish.
Libertè now became animated, and pointing
his spear in the proper direction, made signal
to the man in the stern to give way. He
struck once, twice, without success; but the
third time brought a large fish up on his
spear. It was a sucking carp; a worthless
fish, full of bones, and very watery. However we pursued the remainder, and killed
two more. We advanced nearer the head of
the bay, and at the same time saw two other
lights proceeding from the canoes of Indians
who had visited the neighbourhood, and were
pursuing the same occupation with ourselves.

All of a sudden Libertè again sounded an
alarm, and off we were again in pursuit of a
fish, which I could not for a long time see: a
fine salmon-trout, but of a nature infinitely
wilder than the carp. We chased him like lightning, turning and doubling in his wake, till I
was obliged to hold both sides of the canoe to
keep myself from being thrown out into the

water.   However I caught sight of the fish
every now and then, when he was for a moment still; then he made a dart, and all
again was obscure.   We were some minutes
after him, having lost him, and come upon
him again, but finally he eluded our pursuit,
and made his way into deep water, till the
glimmer of his silver sides was lost in the
lurid yellow gleam that, becoming by rapid
degrees more and more opake, confined to
its very narrow limits our subaqueous prospect.   I changed places with Libertè, with
some risk of being upset, and I took the
spear, kneeling down in the head of the canoe.   (We had regularly replenished our
lights, which burnt out every five minutes or
thereabouts.)   We went back to where we
left the carp, and found them again. I struck
at them several times, but without success.   I
found it not only difficult to hit them, from
the refraction of the water, but impossible,
even had I judged the distance correctly, to
drive the spear, by its long bending handle,
straight forward.   I saw some perch close to

the bottom, and I speared one of them. We were in about ten feet water, and I found it was necessary to aim a foot at least below the object. I had the less difficulty, as they were not in motion. I also saw at the bottom a hideous looking fish, yellow with black spots, the body like that of a snake, with a large head, about a foot and a half long, and somewhat in form resembling the small fish found under stones in running streams in England, and called the miller's thumb. I speared him, and found him so strong, that I verily expected he would have broken the handle of the spear. He was what the Canadians call a cat-fish. In his writhing he had a knack of twisting his supple body like an eel round the spear, and with a force that, considering his size, was quite surprising. He was, of course, not eatable.

We remained out upwards of a couple of hours, when, having expended all our lights, we returned home. Besides the salmon, carp, and perch I have mentioned, there were other sorts of fish in the bay. Among the rest, one or two sorts of bass, a fish thick in shape like the bream, and a small fresh water herring, such as I have seen taken out of Lough Neagh, in the north of Ireland, and where they are called pullen. A small craw-fish was not unfrequent. All the fish however, it must be confessed, were of very inferior quality.

April 22d. The weather was now very good, but the trees bore still their winter appearance. It was past the middle of the day, when I was sitting on a bank above the water's edge, close to the place where I had missed my powder-horn two days before, when I espied it lying at the bottom of the water, and on the verge of a cleft rock. The water was quite smooth, and, in the part where it lay, nearly six feet deep: it appeared to be resting so precariously above the cleft, that the slightest touch might put it out of sight. So, as there was nothing else to be done, I took off all my clothes, and taking the water a few yards away from the place, swam round so as to have it between me and the shore; then diving, I managed to get hold of a piece of projecting rock with one hand, while I secured my prize with the other. The water I was surprised to find by no means cold, considering it had been so short a time released from its covering of ice. It was, in fact, warmer than it would have been at the same season in England.

April 23d. My neighbour, Mr. F——, whose arrival I mentioned on the 5th, had in a very few days, by the help of his axe, settled himself in a very comfortable log-house, a very few hundred yards distant from mine; and he came to me this morning to request me to lend him my canoe to cross the lake to the landing at Holland River, on his way to York. I could not spare my canoe, it was so important an article of my establishment; nor did I like to refuse the poor man; so I determined to go myself and to take him with me. I had several reasons for going to York. Among the rest, my clothes were so torn in pieces that it was almost a matter of necessity to procure a refit; and Libertè, together with Mr. F., who was an able hand at a paddle, could, both together, man the canoe. Mr. F. had intended, I believe, to take his wife with him; but the present plan did not admit of it, for the canoe would hold no more than three persons. The lady, however, was not pleased at remaining at home, and threw obstacles in the way, which the husband overruled, and the voyage was determined on for the next day.

April 24th. At about two o'clock in the afternoon we all got into the canoe—Mr. F., Libertè, and myself. And the two former, at the head and stern, with each a paddle, pulled hard and steadily, so that, keeping in shore all the way, we were soon clear out of the bay. But we had no sooner got completely out of the lee of the land, than we found the wind, which was against us, much stronger than we had expected; so much so, that it would have been unsafe to attempt to stretch across the lake. We therefore kept in shore for about a dozen miles, and then hawling the canoe on the land, we made a fire, before which we broiled some fish, and then lay down before it for the night, which was fortunately, though windy, perfectly dry.

April 25th. At day-light we launched the canoe, and, stretching across the lake, landed at a house situated on the opposite bank, where I got a very tolerable breakfast; and embarking again, we had not been more than an hour on our way before the wind began again to blow so fresh that we could not proceed; and although we were a very little way from the mouth of Holland River, found it impossible to reach it, the waves being so rough. Therefore, in order to wait till the weather should be more calm, we hauled the canoe again on shore; and there we remained on a bare, unsheltered point of land, with the wind blowing a full gale, till six in the evening, when, finding there was no chance of favorable weather, we crept a little way along shore, and prepared again for a bivouac. We were very near the mouth of Holland River, but there was a small bay to cross, too rough for our cranky little vessel.

April 26th. We were in the canoe again

at daylight, and in good time in the morning reached the landing where I had embarked on the 26th of February. This was my first voyage in a birch canoe. The weather was certainly against us, but we had been nearly two days going less than forty miles, and had slept two nights out of doors into the bargain. I had taken my gun with me, and as the weather was very good and the river quite smooth, I shot a few birds on the way. One, a sort of reed-sparrow, the size of a thrush, and of a rich, dead-black plumage; the shoulders of the wings a brilliant scarlet, tempered off with yellow. Its chirp is particularly musical; it clings by its feet to the reeds, and has a bobbing motion of its head and tail when on the wing; the bill quite black, very thick at the upper part, and sharp as a needle at the point. I also shot a dwarf bittern, in all respects like the common English bittern, as to shape, colour, pea-green legs, &c., except as to size, which was very diminutive. As soon as I got out of the canoe I walked eleven miles to Newmarket, where I went to the house of

Mr. Peter Robinson, who was kind enough to endeavour to procure me a conveyance to York.

April 27th.—Although I was in the town of Newmarket, I found it was by no means an easy matter to procure a horse, or indeed any other sort of conveyance. I, therefore, determined to start on foot the next morning.

April 28th to May 3rd.—Having walked thirty miles to York, I went to the house of Mr. C——, where I fared sumptuously during my stay. With regard to myself, nothing had transpired, nor could I get any information relative to the period I was likely to remain in the woods; so, having cased myself in buckram, by the assistance of an honest tailor, I soon became, as far as dress could make me, a better man than I was before. I desired Libertè to meet me the next day at Newmarket, and hired a horse to be ready at an early hour.

May 4th.—Mr. C—— accompanied me on horseback to Newmarket, where we both put up at Mr. Peter Robinson's house. Mr. C—

also undertook to supply me with a good staunch batteau, then lying in Holland River, to take me to Kempenfeldt Bay, and keep there for my use so long as I should remain.

May 5th.—Libertè and I walked together from Newmarket so the landing at Holland River, where I inspected the batteau. It was a sound boat, but very heavy; and as I had not seen Mr. F——, since I left him at this very spot, he having remained at York, there was nobody but Libertè and I to paddle her. I had never had a paddle in my hand, but knowing how to handle an oar, and being anxious to get on, resolved not to delay. Besides, the wind appeared tolerably favourable, and we had a small sail. So, fastening my canoe (which I left here during my journey to York) astern, we both embarked. The wind helped us a good deal; but our course was not straight, so that we had a good deal of hard pulling, which made me very tired, not being used to it. However, before sunset, we arrived at the same house on the banks of the Lake, where I had breakfasted on the morning of the 25th April. I was shewn into a room with a good fire, which, as the evening had set in rather cold, was by no means disagreeable; and prepared to take my supper.

However, before this meal was produced, which, by the way, consisted of nothing more than rashers of bacon and fried eggs, the arrival of an Indian and his canoe was announced; and in a few minutes after, Mrs. F——, the lady whose husband had left her at Kempenfeldt Bay, entered the room. Determined not to remain at home by herself, she had, it appeared, resolved to follow her husband to York, and had arrived thus far under the care of an old Indian, who had brought her across the Lake in his canoe. She no sooner came into the room, than it was evident, by the way she pulled out her pins and placed her feet upon the fender, that she felt herself perfectly at home where she was. I very soon perceived that American customs were likely to prevail, and that unless chance should throw in a third person to interrupt the *tête-à-tête*, we were doomed to pass the evening in each other's company. This not only proved to be the case, but our landlady positively disposed of us in separate beds in opposite corners of the same room, where we remained till the morning. I had nothing to do with the usages of other countries, but really could not help thinking the proceeding altogether rather strange.

I was awakened early in the morning by the busy sounds of a farm-house. The mistress was up, and the maid, and the children, and each had something or other to do. One split logs for the fire, another scrubbed the boards, while the landlady regulated the motions of her troops by scolding and encouraging by turns. She herself had undertaken to whip out the fowls, which had taken possession of the kitchen, and were making their exit with all possible reluctance; cackling, flapping their wings, overturning pewter plates, and finally, after raising all the dust they could, bolting out of the window.

May 6th.—The Canadian Libertè, and I, pursued our voyage early in the morning, and with the assistance of our sail crossed the lake. We then had a great deal of hard pulling. However, soon after midday we hauled the batteau on shore, made a fire, and broiled a large fish I had purchased of the Indian in the morning, after which, being refreshed, we re-embarked, and arrived at my log house, at Kempenfeldt Bay, late in the evening.

May 7th and 8th.—Wishing to explore the woods on the other side of the bay, at sunrise I got into the batteau, taking my gun with me, and having provided myself with provisions for the day, when I had crossed over, sent it back, appointing it to call to take me home at sunset. I rambled about all day, visiting one beautiful and picturesque spot after another, following particularly the course of a small stream unusually romantic. Sometimes the stillness of the scene was interrupted by a cascade: a little farther the sound of the rivulet which produced it would die upon the ear, as its banks widened into those of a placid lake. Coming suddenly upon wild fowl every now and then, I was the more allured to proceed onwards, and I shot several of different sorts, as well as a few partridges and pigeons.

I was at a considerable distance from the bay and had arrived at a sequestered spot, where a basin of resplendent water, almost circular, was sheltered all round by magnificent pines; when my dog suddenly barked, and turning round, I saw an Indian carrying a canoe on his back, approaching the place where I was. He was accompanied by his squaw, and she led by the hand a fine animated little savage, a boy about six years old. A half starved dog, as wild as a fox, accompanied the party. This animal no sooner saw me, than he ran cringing and yelping to the rear, with his tail between his legs, nor could he be prevailed upon, for many minutes, to advance a step nearer. The Indian had brought his canoe to this little lake for the purpose of fishing, and I very readily made him understand that I was anxious to witness his operations. In a few seconds the crazy toppling bark was in the water, the squaw holding it by the head while the man got in with his fish spear, and then stepping in carefully herself, she sat down in the stern with her paddle. The man stood upright, an attitude requiring an extreme nicety of balance, considering the cranky nature of these birch canoes. They are really the most ticklish of all possible vessels. Empty, they are altogether above the water, and do not draw literally more than a couple of inches. When laden, it is not an unusual accident for a man to be thrown overboard out of the vessel, which slips from under him without upsetting, or taking in a drop of water. However, the squaw paddled gently and steadily round the margin of the basin, while the man occasionally struck at fish with his spear. In a few minutes he had taken four or five, for he hardly missed a blow. The direction in which he pointed his spear, and the animated gestures accompanying the action, were signals readily understood by the squaw, and she regulated the course of the canoe and its rate accordingly. And this was done with the utmost silence. The child was left on the bank while his father was pursuing the fish, and I took him by the hand endeavouring to engage his attention, but he would take not the least notice of me, following the canoe with his little eager eyes, as if he already longed in his heart for the privileges of manhood. Every time his father hit a fish, the little fellow could hardly contain himself with joy.

The fish were now brought on shore, and a fire was kindled. The poor lean cur had ventured within a few yards (urged by starvation) for the sake of the entrails of the fish, which, on being thrown to him, he devoured with a voracity really melancholy to see, for he must have been without food a long time. The fish was cut into junks, and these they broiled on the embers, and the dog eat the bones as well as the heads and tails. All was then divided into shares, one for the Indian, another for the squaw, and the third for the child, whom they called " Cawhee ", and each mess was put into a small vessel made of birch bark, out of which they fed themselves with their fingers.

The great utility of the bark of the birch tree is very remarkable. Not only are the canoes in which the Indians trust themselves on lakes sufficiently boisterous, some miles from the shore, made of it, but also all sorts of small cups and dishes. Besides, it burns like pitch; splits into threads which serve for twine; and the filmy part, near the outside, may be written upon in pencil, making no bad substitute for paper. The family had no sooner concluded their repast, than the man took the canoe on his back, and the squaw, having made a bundle of the things, followed, leading the little boy, and they were very soon out of sight and hearing.

I made my way again towards the bay, and as I came upon the banks, a white headed eagle was soaring high in the air. As he floated magnificently above me, I could fancy I distinguished the unrelentless ferocity of countenance that marked his race. Display-ing his expanding wings, he now and then shook his quills with a noise like the flutter of a silken flag in a gale of wind, and he stretched his neck towards the earth as if in defiance of its inhabitants. I fired at him, but the shot glanced from his shield of feathers, and in a few seconds dropped harmlessly into the water.

Returning to the spot where I had appointed to meet the batteau, I found it already there, and, pulling across, it was almost dark when I got home.

May 9th to 18th.—The weather, during these days, was cold and windy, with frosts generally during the night. Vegetation seemed backward, nor was any tinge of green as yet visible on the trees. Working in the forest with my axe on some days, and on others traversing the woods in quest of game, time passed over my head rapidly.

I fell in with an Indian who had three young beavers alive. The little things were the size of pointer puppies of five weeks old, and were just beginning to eat. I felt much inclination to buy them, but the care they required was more than I had it in my power to bestow; I therefore, although with regret, left them to their fate, which was, no doubt, to be speedily eaten by the Indian and his family.

May 19th.—About three o'clock in the afternoon it began to snow heavily, and the ground was covered the rest of the day. My Canadians asserted that they had never remembered snow so late in the season.

May 20th.—This morning the ground was still quite covered with snow, but towards the middle of the day the sun made his appearance and speedily melted it. I was awakened in the middle of the night by the noise of a parcel of wolves, which were yelping close to my house. I was well acquainted with the sound, having once kept a tame wolf for some time, so I listened and found that whatever their object was they were remaining in my neighbourhood. I accordingly dressed myself, and taking my gun from the hooks over the fire, I loaded one barrel with ball, and calling my dog with me, I stole as quietly as I could out of the house. The moon shone bright, and I could have distinguished an object a long way off; however, when I came towards the place where I had heard them, (not above an hundred yards distance,) I could see nothing at all. I had some trouble to keep in my dog, for he was anxious to follow them; however, I kept him still, and remained so myself, and in a few minutes I heard them again, yelping just as they did before, about the same distance from me, quite in another direction. Thither I immediately posted, and was again disappointed; and they repeated the same manœuvre several times afterwards, till it was quite evident that I had no chance whatever of getting a shot at them. They no doubt saw me, and instinctively kept out of shot; so, before I returned to my bed, I gave them a halloo, upon which my dog dashed forward towards them with the most eager alacrity. I was afraid of mischief, and called him back, but Rover was gone, and I called and whistled in vain. He was absent more than five minutes, and came back panting like a badly broken pointer from coursing a hare. I had always believed that dogs had an instinctive dread of the wilder animals, but the above is an instance to the contrary. This dog, a water spaniel, not above the common size, would have hardly been able to throttle a fox; but he certainly had no fear, whatever respect he might have paid to a wolf in close quarters; his experience at least told him that his enemy would run, for he pursued at a reckless rate, probably sure of never over-taking his game.

May 21st.—Flies, for the last few days past, had been making their appearance in increasing numbers; they were already exceedingly troublesome, so much so that the Canadians had begun to wear gauze veils, with which they were all provided during their hours of work. This was a precaution which had never been suggested to me, and, even if it had, probably nothing short of woeful experience would have convinced me of the necessity of using such things. However, matters looked really serious when I found that the tough skins of my labourers were an insufficient defence; and I called to mind what the high-lander had told me in the winter, (" that the flies wad nap a body",) with a regret that I had listened without drawing a moral from the tale. This day, in addition to those before arrived, a small black fly came in clouds, so as to give me neither peace nor rest. The summer, which I had with such eagerness anticipated, was not, I found, about to dispense pleasure without alloy, and the attacks of these winged vermin were a grievous evil. The sun shone clear and hot, and they pitched upon my face in thousands. They got into my eyes and down my throat, and my temples were covered with speckles. They were so voracious that they suffered themselves to be killed where they were, rather than take the trouble to fly away. With my hands I swept them off by hundreds, and legions returned to the charge so as to torment me almost out of my life. All the morning it was impossible to attempt to shoot, and to drive them away was the whole occupation of the day. They were the size of a large flea. Their sting fortunately was not venomous. As the day declined they were less numerous, and two hours before sunset they wholly disappeared. Upon no occasion was I more disheartened than by the grievance I had thus endured. It seemed to threaten so much those little comforts which not only relieved solitude, but even had hitherto rendered my manner of life agreeable.

My enemies had no sooner retired, than I took up my gun rather despondingly, hoping to obtain at least a few moments' tranquillity; and, going to the margin of the bay, I perceived a large flock of wild fowl on the water swimming along close in shore, and I sat down, with my dog by my side, to await their approach. But a little villain of a squirrel, on the bough of a tree close to me, seemed to have determined that even now I should not rest in quiet, for he sputtered and chattered with so much vehemence that he attracted the attention of my dog, whom I could scarcely controul. Meanwhile the birds were coming nearer and nearer, chasing the water

U

insects on their way, stretching forward their necks, splashing, flapping their wings, rubbing their backs with their polls, quacking, fluttering half up out of the water, and then, with a comfortable wriggle of the tail, sitting quietly down again.   With my thumb on the cock of my gun, I was preparing for a double shot; but the " vagrant inattention" of my dog was truly mortifying; he kept his eyes fixed upon the squirrel, now so noisy as to be quite intolerable.   With my hand I made a motion to threaten him, but the little beast actually set up his back and defied me, becoming even more passionate and noisy than before : till, all of a sudden, as if absolutely on purpose to alarm the game, down he let himself drop, plump at once within a couple of yards of Rover's nose.   This was too much for any four-footed animal to bear, so he gave a bounce and sprang at the impertinent squirrel, who, in one second, was safe out of his reach, cocking his tail and shewing his teeth on the identical bough where he had sat before.   Away flew all the wild fowl, and my sport was completely marred. I could not help excusing the dog's error, but my gun went involuntarily to my shoulder to shoot the squirrel.   At the same moment I felt I was about to commit an act of sheer revenge, on a little courageous animal which deserved a better fate. As if aware of my hesitation, he nodded his head with rage, and he stamped his fore paws on the tree; while in his chirruping there was an intonation of sound which seemed addressed to an enemy for whom he had an utter contempt. " What business", I could fancy he said, " had I there, trespassing on his domain and frightening his wife and little family, for whom he was ready to lay down his life?   Could I not find, within these wide woods, one other spot without the pale of his small limited estate?   There he would sit in spite of me and mine, and make my ears ring with the sound of his war whoop, till the spring of life should cease to bubble in his little heart." * * *   And thus he succeeded in driving me away from the spot, and I left him singing the song of triumph, and ever after, as far as I was concerned, in full and complete possession.

May 22d.—I was in my house rather later than usual this morning, for I was busy in preparing a sort of mask of linen for my face, in order to resist, if possible, the attacks of the flies. For some time I had been thinking of this, but I had not any gauze or muslin that would do for a veil, and I had hardly yet imagined a suitable substitute. Now I could no longer delay. My clothes were full of holes, and the flies had read me a lesson, in which their acute reasoning and pointed arguments had prevailed against farther procrastination. As I was just beginning my work, my attention was attracted to the latch of my door, which was lifted up, and at the same moment two very pretty young Indian squaws appeared, by their smiling looks, to be asking admittance to my dwelling.

Even in these uncivilized regions there was nevertheless a spirit of flirtation in their manner, which has existed no doubt throughout all ages, even from the day when, upwards of two thousand years ago, Galatea threw a hard apple at the head of the Roman poet. The minds of both were evidently made up to pay me a visit, though it appeared they were undetermined which of the two ought to walk in before the other; and so the one pushed her friend by the shoulders. Thus, she that was first could not help being pushed, and being pushed, could not help being first. Not much time was expended on the threshold, for their scruples, whatever they might have been, were speedily adjusted, and on tip toes, with a cautious step, they commenced an inquisitive survey of every thing I had, of which my double barrelled gun seemed most to attract their attention. Bound to do the honours of my house, I was equally civil to both, and my civilities had of late been but little in demand. In the wilds where I had lived, civil speeches, compliments, &c. had been frozen up, as it were, like the music in Baron Munchausen's French horn, and now I had occasion for all at once. I continued to hold an intelligible conversation, although neither of the damsels could speak a word of English, and I was equally ignorant of their language. Their quickness of apprehension however was such, that I was readily understood. One of them took the needle and sewed the strings to the mask I had been making, which very much amused them both. And they recommended me to rub my face with grease, by way of a certain defence against all sorts of flies. Disagreeable as it may seem, I resolved, in case of the failure of my present plan, to follow their advice.

After a sufficiently long morning visit, my guests seemed at last anxious to depart, and I accompanied them to the edge of the bay, where they had left their canoe. They were, it seemed, without other company, and, stepping lightly into their little vessel, they paddled away round a point of land between the spot on which I was standing and the head of the bay. They waved their hands as long as they were in sight. I knew nothing of their history, and I regretted that I might never see them again.   Such, indeed, was the case !

In point of clothes and appearance they were superior to any I had seen of their race, and in face and figure seemed to me really beautiful. They had silver ornaments in their ears, a necklace each of blue beads, and quantities of scarlet serge disposed about their dress instead of riband.

May 23rd.—During the last two days the trees had changed considerably, owing to the warm weather ; and now, for the first time, they might fairly be said to be green.   Several boat-loads of stores arrived from York, across lake Simcoe, for the post of Michilimackinac, and were landed at the head of the bay.

May 24th.—For reasons connected with my duty, I resolved to change my residence to the head of the bay, and therefore set the Canadians at work there to make me a log-house.   I spent a great part of the day on the spot, not only in determining the situ-

ation, but in waiting to see the first logs laid
on the ground.

May 25th.—As I was out shooting I saw a
loon swimming towards a point of land where
I could easily conceal myself, so I repaired
thither for that purpose. A loon is a very
large description of diver, but so cautious
and wary, and at the same time so quick in
turning himself under the water, that, though
I had shot at several, I had never been able to
kill one. He is covered with small spots like
those of the starling, and is the size of a large
goose. He has a wild, anxious gait as he
is swimming, constantly turning his head
from side to side as if to be upon his guard
against an enemy; and his cry is as wild as
his looks, for it exactly resembles the whooping of an owl. I had arrived at the place,
and the bird was approaching. Now and then,
as he came on, he stretched his long neck for
several seconds under the water, looking for
small fish; and when he had nothing better
to do, he turned his head round, in order to
tickle his tail with his bill. I felt myself sure

of him; and, choosing the latter attitude as the one in which he was the most exposed, I let fly when he was within thirty yards of me. My gun went quick as lightning; but the loon was still quicker, and, scrambling over out of sight, came up again in a few seconds perfectly unhurt, and whooping as if to mock my attempt upon his life. I never again shot at one of these birds. The Indians shoot them frequently; which is very surprising, considering that their guns are of coarse Birmingham manufacture, and their powder very indifferent. They kill, nevertheless, extremely long shots, putting in a large quantity of powder and very little shot; and they have a way of enticing the loons by a call and a red rag at the end of a stick, which they practise with great success.

May 26th.—My new log-house was not finished, but I resolved to move my quarters, as the day was fine, at once; and so, having put all my things into the batteau, I was going to walk along shore through the wood, when I saw an Indian passing by in his canoe,

and hailed him. He was making his way towards the head of the bay whither I was going, and I asked him to take me on board,—
not so much for convenience as from curiosity.
He pulled in shore immediately, and was
amused at my request, seeming particularly
entertained at the clumsy manner in which I
got in. His family consisted of the squaw, a
little girl of about ten years old, another of
six, and a third of four; and as I was just
going to sit down in the bottom of the canoe,
the squaw gave me a hard pull by the coat,
and, removing a dirty blanket, uncovered the
features of a little infant bound, after their
fashion, very securely upon a board : and this
made the fourth child of the party. The
squaw was going to remove it to where she
sat in the stern, but I gave her to understand
that I would nurse it as we went along ; and
I took hold of the wooden frame and laid it
on my knees.

It was admirable to see how well the little
thing was secured from harm, and how quiet
and contented it seemed in its state of impri-

sonment. Protected from the weather by clothes in numerous folds, a circular piece of wood formed a guard for its head, and altogether it was the same as taking hold of a fiddle, so tight was it bound upon its wooden frame. With its arms and legs in a state of confinement, the little being could only move its wandering eyes, which, together with its tiny trembling lips, told the tale of its tender age. I could not help considering the mode of treating the infant savage, of which I had an example now before me, more worthy than I should have imagined of being placed in comparison with that adopted among civilized people; and certainly, whatever may be said against it, it possesses some advantages over our mode of nursing. During the first few weeks of infancy, when the very bones have not acquired their proper consistence, and the unclosed skull hangs a dead weight upon the body, the Indians bind, as it were, the tender plant to a stake, to be protected in its growth from that violence of motion, those twists and strains, which with us confessedly lead to some of our most dreadful disorders.   Here was a child happy as it could be, and as warm, without a pin in its whole dress to torment it, capable of enjoying exercise, and of being moved from place to place over land and water, without the slightest stress upon its pliant limbs.

The canoe, paddled by the squaw sitting in the stern, glided quietly along within a few feet of the shore; and the Indian stood up all the time in the head looking out for fish.   The sun shone bright upon the water, nevertheless I could not discern one, although he struck at some several times on the way.   He killed three bass, turning round the spear each time to the squaw in order that she might extricate the fish.   The least unsteadiness on his part might have precipitated the whole party, children and all, into the water; but he kept his balance with such extraordinary certainty, that I very soon lost all apprehension of the possibility of such an accident, and we arrived at the head of the bay, where we all got out.

The Indian and his family were on their route to Lake Huron, and they had now eight miles to travel to the Notawasorga River, all which distance it was necessary to carry the canoe. He immediately commenced preparations to take it on his back, and for this purpose he fixed a broad strip of birch bark to the centre thwart, making the ends fast to each opposite gunwale. The thwart then rested on his shoulders, and, having placed a piece of bark doubled under it to prevent its galling, he contrived to lay the greater part of the weight of the canoe on his forehead by means of the strip of bark, which at the same time kept all steady. The canoe once poised, was nearly horizontal, and on he marched, caring little for the weight. Before he set off, however, the squaw stuck his gun and the fish spear under the thwarts, and then made up her own bundle. She carried this, much in the same way, by means of a forehead strap; and on the top of it the little Δεσμώτης rode upon its board, having been first safely tied by the little girl with strips of bark, so that it could not possibly fall off. The three children brought up the rear, and the whole party soon disappeared.

May 27th.—I went out in the evening to spear fish with one of the Canadians. He speared eight fish of different sorts, one of them a remarkably fine salmon trout. I found my canoe grew very leaky for want of the proper sort of turpentine for paying the seams. It was of so delicate a make that it required not only the greatest care on my part, but more than I could give it from want of experience and knowing how to handle it properly. I saw it was approaching towards its end, and in a little time would be good for nothing, and, as the batteau was too unwieldy for my purpose, it was time to think of supplying its place; and therefore I resolved to set about making, with the assistance of the Canadians, a log-canoe.

May 28th.—I went out into the woods to look for a tree suitable to the object I had in view, and very soon pitched upon one. It was a fine white pine, and its girth, between three and four feet from the ground, was eleven feet three inches. I began immediately to cut it down with my axe, and was some time about it, working very sharply, and was a good deal tormented all the while by mosquitoes, for the tree grew in a low, swampy place, where there were a great many. I killed a few occasionally upon my face and wrists, though I was too eagerly employed to care much about them. At last the tree fell to the ground, and I left the spot, when I soon found that I had reason to repent my visit to the mosquitoes; for their bite was so acrid and poisonous, that before the middle of the night I was in a state of actual misery, and felt a degree of inflammatory itching so intense that, bemoaning my hard fate, I was forced to exert my utmost resolution to enable me to endure it. My eyes were closed, and my wrists were knotted and swollen to double their natural size.

May 29th.—I got up in the morning a hideous figure, as far as the only piece of looking-glass I had (a circular bit of about a

couple of inches' diameter, fixed in the lid of a
little box,) could inform me. My eyes were
both black, and my cheeks puffed out; but
the pain and heat were gone. These mosquitoes are attached to particular situations in
the woods : they like wet, swampy places,
and remain there till some unlucky person
visits them; otherwise they do not go out of
their way " en masse" to infest people. This
little bit of natural history I have ever since
remembered.

May 30th.—I had happened to break one
of the iron spikes of my fish spear. This day
I met an Indian in the woods, who spoke
English tolerably well; so I asked him if he
had one that he could sell me. He said, "No;
but may be me make one very good :" and
so we went together to my house to get the
old one, and at the same time he took hold
of my double-barrelled gun, and began to
examine that. It had met with a trifling accident,—a small piece of wood having been
split off between the lock and the barrel; and
the moment he saw it he said, " Master, In-

dian man mend that too." As I intended to stand by him all the time to prevent his doing mischief, I told him he should. He accordingly set to work with great ingenuity. He forged the iron of the spear in my fire, beating it with a hammer against a large stone; and he made a very neat splice to mend the gunstock, which he cemented with a sort of glue he carried in his pouch, and made by boiling the bones of fish.

I tried to get him to explain how it was that he found his way in the woods; but, like the rest of these people, let the questions be stated to them how they may, their ideas are so limited, that they cannot be brought to reason upon the most trifling operation of the mind. He told me of a beaver dam, as it is called, in the neighbourhood: a work erected by the animals for the purpose of rearing their young, and where they live in considerable numbers. It was about four miles off, on a small river which crossed the road I had travelled towards Lake Huron; so that I understood, by the direction he gave me, exactly where to go. I was very curious to see the work of these wonderful creatures, and would have taken the Indian immediately with me as a guide, but he could not stay. In the evening I went by myself, and, when I came to the river, I followed the banks till I had nearly, as I thought, arrived at the spot. There appeared what I fancied the remains of an old wooden bridge, made of the trunks of small trees, and broken in the middle. The stream was moderately rapid, and immediately below the bridge there was a turn in the river, so that it formed a still pool of rather large dimensions. I pursued the course of the river for some distance farther, but finding no signs of the beaver habitation I had come to see, I returned home. Upon talking to the Canadians, I found that the bridge which I had taken for the work of man was literally that of the beavers; that the place had been deserted by them for some years, therefore the remains only of their works were to be seen. The structure was wonderful: the work was carried on under the water as well as above it;

and the trees were of such a size, and laid with such ingenuity one upon another to oppose the current, that one would have thought that nothing short of human skill and science could have contrived it.

May 31st.—I went to see the Canadians at work. They were employed in making a sort of wharf, with pine logs, to facilitate the landing of the boats. There was an old man among them, an English Canadian, whom they called Mr. Weller; a very steady character, but so very grave and free from every thing at all like fun, that he was a continual source of merriment to the rest, while, on his part, nothing at all disturbed his tranquillity. The men had all on their veils, and the flies were buzzing in vast quantities about them, while Mr. Weller alone was without any sort of covering on his face. Accordingly, I told him to trim the pine that lay in the swamp where I had been so miserably stung, and calling him away, accompanied him to the spot. The mosquitoes were in a moment at their post, and I could hardly preserve my

x 2

gravity, as I began, by flattering his skill, to propose to him to fashion the tree into the form of a canoe. He readily acceded to the undertaking, and I left him hard at work. In about a couple of hours I returned to see how he was going on. As the day was excessively hot, the situation had one advantage; that of being cool. Long before I arrived, I heard the blows of Mr. Weller's axe falling steadily one after another, and as I approached him, there he was, without coat, waistcoat, or hat! His shirt collar was open, and he was slashing away just as if there was no such thing as a mosquitoe in North America, although they were swarming about his head like bees, and absolutely standing on his hair. " You are a little troubled here with mosquitoes, Mr. Weller," said I. So he drew himself up to answer, and after spitting out the little bits of wood that had flown off the point of his axe into his mouth,—" Yes," said he, " they are pretty considerable thick, but they don't *hort* me much with their bills, if they didn't keep on whizzling so about a body's head :" and then he looked at his large fore-finger, and seemed to be thinking. He told me " he had been married thirty-five years, that his wife was much respected, and did a great deal of business." " What business ?" said I. " What business?" said he, " why she rides." Still I was in ignorance, till I found, that for an old woman to ride, meant the same as to say, that she practised the profession of a midwife. And so I left Mr. Weller, who worked the remainder of the day without making the least complaint.

June 1st.—One of the men brought in an animal, which he had killed in the woods, and which he called a wood chuck, or ground hog, about the size of a Chinese pig half grown, and resembling a Guinea pig in shape and species. They burrow in the ground, are particularly fat, and so slow of foot as to be easily overtaken. They are said to be good eating. I shot a bird a little smaller than a thrush, with a red breast and head, and back of a bright blue. The weather was now moderately cool, and similar in its variety to that in England at the same time of year.

Mr. Weller had finished the canoe before sunset, and I had her brought down to the water and launched. But she was so lop-sided as to be quite unserviceable in her present state. To remedy this was found to be no easy matter. Large chips were cut off with the broad axe, which produced various changes of her position on the water; but the changes were all wrong, and do what we would, we could not lay her quite horizontal. Besides, the wood was green and heavy, and she sunk by far too low. Finally, we nailed a small slab of cedar on her side to produce an equilibrium; but, after all, she looked so extremely awkward, and the case was so hopeless a one, that I was not only obliged to abandon her altogether, but was at considerable additional trouble to fill her with large stones and sink her, for she looked so ugly that I could not bear to see her. So I was again obliged to have recourse to my birch canoe, the seams of which one of the men contrived to pay tolerably well with turpentine, and she became again fit for service.

The wild fowl had now nearly all departed, and spearing fish was almost my only amusement. The partridges too were gone. In fact, the birds had all begun to breed. Instead of my gun, therefore, I generally carried my axe in my hand, by means of which I made myself tired enough to feel comfortable during the very short time I sat still. One or other of the men was frequently bringing in fish caught in various ways, by angling, trolling, &c. I had plenty for breakfast and dinner. With reference to past times, therefore, a comparison naturally suggested itself in favour of the present hour. I found the solitude of my life every day less irksome; and an additional source of interest rose up more and more in the objects around me. In cutting down trees I had learnt to make them fall which way I pleased, and I was continually engaged by thus increasing the natural beauties of my situation, and removing the obstacles which blocked up my favourite paths. I extended my walks, by marking the trees in a particular way, as I went, so that I could wander far from my home and in perfect confidence of not losing my way.

June 2d.—The weather to-day was clear and warm. I walked a long way from home, and had pursued a straight line, over ground altogether new to me. I came at last to a ravine, where an unusual extent of open space presented itself, covered at the same time with lovely verdure. The charred trunks of the trees bore testimony of the cause, and it was evident that the part of the forest I was in had been destroyed a few years before by fire. Thus, the large trees had been consumed, and the ashes had given birth to a rich growth of shrubs, now wearing the cheerful green of spring, and enlivened by a profusion of wild flowers, creeping out of the earth, and disposing themselves in the delicate arrangement of nature everywhere around them. In this sweet shrubbery, there was the birch and maple, (the token of an improved soil,) while wild currant and gooseberry bushes, in rich abundance, tufted the banks of a little stream of clear water. I naturally stopped to look around me, and sat down quite delighted at so charming a spot.

Beautiful birds were drinking, and splashing themselves in the water, and gaudy butterflies, of a very large size, were fanning the air with their yellow and black wings. At this moment, a little blazing meteor shot like a glowing coal of fire across the glen; and I saw, for the first time, with admiration and astonishment, what in a moment I recognized to be the greatest of Nature's beauties of the feathered race, that resplendent living gem, the humming bird! Buzzing like an humble bee, which it exactly resembled in its flight and sound; like it, it sprang through the air, by a series of instantaneous impulses, tracing angle after angle, with the velocity of lightning; till poised above its favourite flower, all motion seemed lost in its very intensity; and

the humming sound alone certified to the ear
the rapid vibration of wing by which it supported its little airy form. I was never more
excited to wonder than by this little creature,
so unexpected was its appearance, and so much
more did it resemble a splendid shining insect
than a bird.

The place I was in seemed fairy land complete, and it was matter of regret, that Πυρὸς
ἡ μαλερὰ γνάθος, the *voracious jaw of fire*,
had not more often, as in the present instance,
effected such changes of scenery in the neighbourhood of my dwelling; for it is remarkable, considering every Indian and traveller
usually lights his fire against the trunk of
some prostrate tree, and leaves it burning, that
conflagration should not be more general and
frequent. As it is, however, few summers
pass away without instances of such accidental
combustion, (one, indeed of late years, most
serious and fatal in its consequences,) when
volumes of smoke, proceeding from a spot distant and unknown, envelope in thick fog the
inhabitants of the settled parts of the country,

who pursue their daily avocations without en-
quiring from whence the winds have wafted
the gloomy curtain, although the air is ob-
scured and darkened as if by a natural mist.

June 3rd.—This evening, as the weather
was particularly fine, I went out in my birch
canoe to spear fish, and narrowly escaped a
serious accident. I had taken one of the Canadians with me as well as my servant, and
was kneeling down in the bow of the canoe,
where I had a large heap of pieces of birch
bark split into the proper shape, from which
I occasionally replenished the light in the cleft
pole which overhung the water. We went
on paddling round the margin of the bay, till
I had taken two or three fish. But, some
how or other, just as we happened to be
making across from one point to another, and
were in deep water, a little bit of the fire fell
unluckily among the magazine of combusti-
bles, and the whole in a moment was in a
blaze, together with my check linen shirt, for
I had on neither coat nor waistcoat. I soon
extinguished the fire which was destroying my

shirt, but not before my hair and eyebrows were a good deal singed; and working on, by very great exertion I put out the fire altogether. But my hand and right arm were blistered, and I was very near giving up the point, and jumping out of the canoe to swim ashore. The whole business occupied but a very few seconds from the time that the fire was blazing twice as high as my head as I knelt, till we were left glimmering in the dark like an expended Catherine wheel on the water. The fishing was quite put a stop to for the evening, and as it was too late to procure fresh lights instead of those which had been consumed or spoilt, nothing was left but to paddle home.

June 4th.—I saw two very pretty Indian damsels busily employed, broiling fish over a fire they had made on the margin of the bay. Each of them carried a gun, and their canoe was fastened to a large stone. A fish spear was lying in the canoe, also a large salmon trout, which apparently had been just taken. They were gaily dressed, and their cheeks marked with stripes of red paint as if they

were prepared for some festivity. I proposed
to buy the fish, but they were so unaccount-
ably shy that I could not prevail upon them
to listen to a word I had to say; nor by sign
or hieroglyphic could I make the least impression. They ran into the forest, leaving
the fish to broil by itself. So I went away,
and left them to their repast. Afterwards I
discovered that they were living under the
protection of one of the gentlemen of the
North-west Company, and that, notwithstanding the extreme propriety of conduct for which
I had given them credit, they were in fact no
better than they should be.

After this, I was in the interior of the forest,
and I chanced to sit down. My dog was
with me, but had wandered away, for I had
not my gun with me, and took therefore little
pains to restrain him. I heard the sticks
crack close behind me and thought it was he,
but a moment afterwards saw a large long-
legged wolf which had passed within a few
feet of me. With his head and tail low, he
was going a lurching, stealthy trot. When I
saw him he had got about ten yards from me

but he did not look behind him or quicken his pace, but leaped easily over a fallen tree, and was immediately out of sight. Had I my gun with me, instead of my axe, I could have readily shot him.

June 5th to 15th.—The weather, during the whole of this period, was very like that of England; variable, but equally temperate in the extremes. The voracity of the flies, however, was beyond all controul. They were a very plague. Different sorts were ushered into existence, and in a few days replaced by others; bands of unconquerable guerrillas, which harassed and tormented me without mercy. There was a day fly, and a night fly; for the mosquitoe shouldered his arms as soon as the others went to their rest, making up in his weapon, his deficiency in numbers. So bad, indeed, are the mosquitoes, that I have no doubt whatever, that were a man to be exposed to them for the space of an hour without his clothes, they would absolutely sting him to death.

Boat loads of government stores were now arriving, as well as those of the North-west

Company, on the way to Lake Huron, and the margin of the bay began to be a scene of active bustle.   The house of the Canadians (a member of whose mess my servant had been long since enrolled) was crowded with casual lodgers, and it was with difficulty that I could now keep my own house to myself.   I had been in the habit of doing as much as I could for myself; and as I lived almost wholly on fish, I very often cut it into junks and broiled it with my own hands.   Still my servant had quite enough to do, for he washed my clothes, baked my bread, cut birch bark in the woods for lights, went out fishing, and led a life, not solitary like mine, but joyous in the extreme.   Too much so, though his habitual sobriety as yet resisted the deleterious spirits, called whiskey in the country, which the new comers dispensed among the Canadian labourers.   Long after I had retired to rest at night, I heard the bursts of carousal and jollity, with a regret to think of the total change of affairs, and that my days of tranquillity had too soon passed away.

SUMMER JOURNEY FROM LAKE SIMCOE TO QUEBEC,

BY THE FALLS OF NIAGARA AND THE RAPIDS OF THE ST. LAWRENCE.

June 16.—THIS morning I received letters from York announcing my liberation, and conveying to me instructions to proceed thither on my way to Quebec. The intelligence gave me great pleasure, and I immediately commenced active preparations for my departure. Little, indeed, I had to prepare, and that little was most willingly undertaken. Mr. F—— had returned some time since, with his wife, from York, and, hearing of my intended movement, came to me to volunteer to take a paddle in the batteau, to which I acceded. The wife again remonstrated, however we left her behind; and this arrangement Mr. F—— was, I found, upon any reasonable excuse, always ready to agree to.

The man who was the bearer of my letters,

had been sent to take charge of some stores which had been forwarded to Kempenfeldt Bay, and he had brought with him his wife and a little infant child. They had slept out of doors the night preceding, and the woman and baby had both suffered severely from the flies. The poor child's head was miserably swollen, and the good looks of the mother were entirely destroyed by red knobs all over her face. No wonder the poor creature was in a peevish humour, for besides these sufferings, and the loss of beauty, the most severe of all was disappointment; as she had been quite deceived in the accounts of the place to which her husband had brought her. As I was to be off in two hours, I gave up my house with a good grace to her immediately, but in return she abused every thing in it, so that I was happy to keep out of her way; and more happy still, when, with Mr. F—— and one of the Canadians, just before I was stepping into the batteau, I saw, for the last time, her poor husband at the extremity of his wits to find argument to satisfy her remonstrances, and whip away the flies with a little green bough at the same time.

It was about four o'clock when we went on board; the evening was delightfully fine, and the little wind that blew was directly in our favour. We hoisted our small sail, which became gently distended before I lost sight of a few honest faces who came to the water's edge to witness my departure. " Bon voyage" was more than once repeated, I am sure, with sincerity, and more than once I was recalled from my musing by the rude twitch, with which something or other on which I had heedlessly seated myself, was jerked from under me.

Moments of sudden excitement are invariably succeeded by those of seriousness approaching to melancholy, as if the mind had convicted itself of error in having yielded to the delusion of happiness; and now in the eager anticipation of change, aided by the exertion of a few hours' active preparation, the showers of the rainbow had been forgotten, while the colours alone had presented themselves to the senses. New scenes of life were before me, and I was at that moment commencing a journey, which would probably finish, and that before any distant period, in England. I was leaving a spot, where, however I might have accommodated my habits to circumstances, if I had suffered no real grievances, I had unquestionably enjoyed but few solid comforts. Variety was before me; transition from place to place, from object to object; I was again to mix in that general intercourse with the world, without which the choicest gifts of Providence are vapid; and still, in spite of all this, it was not without feelings of real regret, amounting to a depression of spirits, that the well known trees and points of land on each side of the bay, one after another, receded from my view, and gradually, in succession, became lost in the distance. Such is the natural attachment to any spot, however rude, which can be called home! All the difficulties and inconveniences of my life were in a moment forgotten, as my heart whispered adieu to each particular object, as to a friend or acquaintance with whose image the association of happy hours was intimately blended. Let those learn (and many there are who might profit by the lesson) who, having within their possession home and its enjoyments, know not how to appreciate the blessing; how possible it is to fly to the forest without finding solitude, and that a lonely uncultivated spot is in itself capable of creating an interest sufficient to dispose the mind to true happiness and content.

We were soon at the mouth of the bay, and making a good passage across Lake Simcoe. The sun had set, and as we skirted the shore the fire flies were sparkling in glittering swarms among the boughs of the trees which overhung the water's edge. Hitherto I had not seen any of these insects in the country, and I thought them larger and more brilliant than any I had met with in other climates. The wind, which had been all along very gentle, now became quite lulled. The men accordingly took to the paddles, and, keeping in shore, pulled on at a steady rate; and so we proceeded smoothly during the silent hours that passed away, while the whooping of the night birds, and the croaking of deep mouthed frogs, bore sole testimony to the existence of animated nature.

June 17th.—As the pale light of morning gleamed upon the lake, large water hawks, the colour of herons, were to be seen upon their chosen station, and from the craggy stump of a decayed tree, watching for their prey with eyes intently fixed upon the water. And kingfishers, the size of pigeons, slate-coloured with black heads, would plump like stones in pursuit of the small fish that appeared upon the surface. As the day broke we approached the mouth of Holland river, disturbing various sorts of wild fowl as we passed along the banks, till the ruddy light of the sun shed a glowing hue upon the surrounding objects.

It was a fine summer's morning, and I was regretting that my gun was packed up, although we had very few miles to proceed to the landing, when a fine mallard, which had risen out of the reeds, made its flight suddenly over our batteau. Terrified at the unexpected encounter, he turned suddenly, and at the same instant the report of a gun sounded close by us. Nothing of life remained as he fell hurled, by the impulse of his flight, with increased velocity upon the water! There was something so unlooked for in the fate of the bird, that it was really a subject for reflection; when a canoe, with two young smart squaws in it, darted past us, and one of these immediately picked it up.

They wore men's hats, of shining coarse felt, and jackets and petticoats, of glossy blue cloth, ornamented with red serge. And I immediately recognized my two friends, whom I had seen a few days before broiling the fish in the woods at Kempenfeldt Bay. Their protector, the North-west gentleman, was I do not know where, while the damsels were pursuing this roaming life, more memorable perhaps on account of its economy than its morality. Here was an establishment wherein the means of conveyance, as well as the poulterer and fishmonger were provided, in the shape of a canoe, a Birmingham gun, and a fish spear. A little brick-dust served the purpose of rouge, and sturdy blue cloth superseded the more flimsy articles of millinery.

The men who had been paddling all night were jaded and tired, and the squaw who had killed the mallard, having loaded her gun, took her seat opposite to her companion; and they pulled their canoe along at an astonishing rate, twisting and turning with great velocity and skill. They were particularly diverted at the appearance of our batteau, which was a heavy unwieldy vessel, and, being in high spirits and full of mischief, they amused themselves by quizzing the men; first passing us like a shot, then dropping astern and going round us, till, seeing some object which attracted their attention, they left us in eager pursuit towards the lake, and we saw them no more.

Having breakfasted at a house on the banks of the river, I would have hired a horse, or any sort of conveyance, to enable me to proceed; but that was altogether out of the question.: so, leaving my servant with the Canadian who was to carry my baggage, I set out on foot, on my way to York. I was not averse to walking alone, and I went silently off, while Mr. F—— and the host were driving a hard bargain for a pig. The day became intolerably hot, and at the end of twenty-five miles I came to a house which looked so comfortable that I resolved to remain there for the night; and after the rough life I had been leading, every thing looked particularly neat and tidy. On the way I had picked up a land tortoise, as it was walking slowly across the road, not far from the river. Soon after I had arrived, my servant and the Canadian came in with my baggage, Mr. F—— not having brought his negotiation to a conclusion.

June 18th.—I walked (twenty-two miles) the remainder of the way to York, along a wide earthy road, fenced off on each side by the American rail fence, and where traffic and a good even substratum of stone were altogether wanting to bring it towards perfection. Although summer had now re-established her reign, a heavy sameness prevailed over the face of the country, and in the short space between the road and the forest, the naked stumps of trees standing in the ground, gave a desolate appearance to the fields on either side.

I saw a number of yellow birds, such as I had not met with in the woods. The common English martin is to be seen here, forming its nest in the hollow trees, of the minute fibres of roots strongly cemented together, so as to make a compact vessel as tight as a China cup.

June 19th to 27th.—Previously to proceeding to Quebec, I had proposed to myself to visit the Falls of Niagara, and having heard of a vessel about to sail for Fort George, I engaged a passage on board her, but her departure was postponed from day to day, during which time my stay was made agreeable by the kindness and hospitality of Mr. C——, at whose house I resided in the interval.

June 28th.—The distance from York, the

capital of Upper Canada, to Fort George, at the mouth of the Niagara river, is thirty miles. At six in the evening I went on board the Jane, a schooner of fifty tons, and we immediately set sail. There was so little wind that we were all night on Lake Ontario, and the births in the vessel were so bad, that, as the night was mild and fine, I preferred lying on the deck in my clothes, to occupying the best of them.

June 29th.—At nine o'clock in the morning we arrived at Fort George, when Mr. B—— was not only kind enough to invite me to his house during my stay, but lent me a horse to ride to the Falls of Niagara, now sixteen miles distant. No time was expended in delay, and so soon as I had breakfasted, my foot was in the stirrup. I was scarcely out of the town, when I was surprised and pleased at the totally different appearance of the country, to that of any part of North America I had yet visited. That the road to the Falls of Niagara should be one of considerable traffic, and better, in consequence, than the other roads in the country, is not to be wondered at: I could fancy myself transported to a cultivated country in Europe, and on the high road towards some opulent city. As I rode parallel to the Niagara river, which rolled its course on the left hand below me, through a rich ravine, whose elevated banks were covered with ornamental trees and shrubs, I called to mind the banks of the Garonne in the south of France, to which the country bore a striking resemblance. The rich diversity of foliage which prevailed on every side, was a kindly relief to the eye, so long overwhelmed by the prevalence of the dismal black pine, and it now dwelt with grateful delight on the abundant variety of nature, disposing in tasteful succession the wild peach, cherry, sassafras, hiccory, aspen, sycamore, &c.

The roar of Niagara already was distinctly audible, and I saw the cloud of vapour, which, hanging over its verge, like a white pillar in the heavens, pointed towards the chief wonder of the earth!

I rode on till I came to the inn where I

was to leave my horse, and taking a guide with me, proceeded on foot. We descended towards the river, crossing some fields covered with high dry grass, with a rich bottom of clover and thyme. My guide cautioned me to beware of rattlesnakes, which he said were numerous just where we were. None, however, did I see or hear.

On our way towards the Table Rock, we were less than a mile from the Falls, when a sight burst upon the view which I was not prepared to expect—that mighty, rolling mass of water, which above the cascade, rushes onwards, furiously foaming with a velocity tremendously increased to its verge; for the Niagara River, hurried through its lacerated channel, spreads itself over an inclined plane of considerable declivity and magnificent expanse. For the space of a mile before it reaches the Falls, islands and shoals obstruct its course, and black rocks protrude their rugged summits in defiance of the surge: monuments to man of an event which the brief span of his memory has failed to re-

cord. That jarring shock, when the river
yielding its rived banks to the torrent's force,
first bounded from the verge of the precipice! When, with impulse instantaneous, the
stupendous cataract, generated in the convulsion of conflicting torrents, first thundered
into being!

With the strongest anticipation of a spectacle, the very grandest of Nature's efforts, I
was, on my arrival, utterly unprepared for the
splendour of the reality. I had reached the
Table Rock, and the volume of tumbling waters,
their deafening sound, unceasing descent, the
reverberation of the mass below, driving to
the very skies its steaming vapour,—all combined to produce unusual sensations of wonder
and awe. Chaos seemed before me! My ears
were confounded; my sight was dazzled by
whirling eddies, and the everduring liquid
arch, preserving from generation to generation
its palpable figure, formed of particles, myriads upon myriads of which, for the very
minutest portion of a second must have remained suspended each in its place, to per-

form its ordained function in the scale of creation.

Thus eternity obtruded itself on the imagination, wonderfully, infinitely divisible!

Below, and within a very few yards of the abyss, a heavy stillness pervaded the whole surface of the river for a wide extent, as if paralysis had succeeded the violence of the shock; but the milky whiteness of the water bore testimony to the laboured heavings of the current underneath, hurrying along in an overpowering stream towards Lake Ontario. At a distance of five miles from the Falls, the celebrated whirlpool, attracting the largest floating bodies within its vortex, holds its unceasing struggle with the stream, which becomes afterwards gradually more and more placid. At Queen's Town, which is four miles farther, it is still extremely rapid; but after a short distance, and before it empties itself into the lake, it has assumed a quiescent and a tranquil course; nor does any turbid appearance remain, to convey the slightest idea of proximity to the cataract of Niagara.

June 30th.—As it was now my object to proceed to Quebec, by the rapids of the St. Lawrence, I engaged a passage in an American schooner, of fifty tons, which was proceeding in ballast to Sodus, (a port 120 miles distant on the American side of the lake,) there to take in cargo, and sail forthwith to Kingston.

July 1st.—I got on board at six o'clock in the evening, and we immediately weighed anchor. The births and accommodation were uncommonly good. The weather was mild and temperate, and we had a gentle favourable breeze.

July 2d.—At five o'clock in the afternoon we made the port of Sodus, after an extremely pleasant passage. Sodus is a neat country village, situated at the head of a beautiful bay, which forms an excellent harbour for shipping in all weathers. The shores of the lake are hereabouts remarkably bluff, and as the eye glances from the craggy summits of the cliffs to the wide expanse of waters which wash their base, there is no feature in the whole prospect which serves to distinguish a difference between this noble fresh water lake and the ocean itself.   The short, light green wave reminded me of the Bristol Channel and other inland seas.   Having landed, I went to the Troopville Inn, kept by Captain Wickham, of the United States Militia, and here I was to remain till the vessel should be laden.   An unexpected delay, however, seemed likely to take place, for on the 4th of July, the next day but one, was to be celebrated the festival of American Independence, on which occasion a country ball was to be held at Captain Wickham's house, when, as a matter of course, business stood still.

July 3d.—The vessel had now nearly half her cargo on board; and I prevailed upon the master to lend me his boat, in which, attended by a couple of stout Yankee seamen, I passed the evening in rowing about in the bay of Sodus.   A finer piece of water can hardly be imagined.   The most delicate shrubs fringed its banks to the water's edge, and the winding shore broken by creeks and

inlets, furnished store of incessant variety.
We were at one time struggling over shoals
and through reeds, then breaking forth again
into a wide expanse of clear water, where
turtles were to be seen in great numbers, floating on the surface. These creatures were
extremely wild, always disappearing long before we approached them. Their egg-shells
were lying about the sand on the shore in
great quantities.

July 4th.—Captain W—— and all his
family were in the greatest possible bustle the
whole of the morning, in making preparations
for their company. In the mean time I walked
out for a few hours over a country, under a
degree of cultivation such as I had not seen for
a long time, and where the fields, hedges, and
stiles made me almost fancy I was in England.
On my return, the people of the house, without
intending to be uncivil, were extremely rude;
nor could I prevail upon them to prepare any-
thing for my dinner. I got a piece of a cold
meat pudding, out of which, those who had
gone before me had made so judicious a selec-

z

tion, that very little remained but bones and pieces of fat. However, there was soon something else to think about, for the people began to arrive, consisting of young farmers, dressed in coats of glossy blue cloth, with broad white buttons, and rosy damsels, in white calendered gowns, somewhat rumpled by having been packed too close in their carts or whiskeys during the journey. Some came in these carriages, and others on foot, till a large room below was quite full, and they all began to dance.

The fiddler sat on a chair placed upon a large table, playing country dances, and roaring out the figure. There was not an old person in the room to direct the flock, which was noisy and riotous beyond measure.

About three o'clock I went down to the water's edge, where there were a great many small vessels made fast to the wharf; and, as they impeded the landing of people from small boats, those parties which were making their way to the ball by water, clambered up and walked on shore over a plank, which was laid down for the purpose. As I was looking at the people landing in this way one after another, a tidy little woman, not more than thirty years of age, and very smart, was passing the plank, when her foot slipped, and she fell into the water between the vessel and the wharf, and I had a great deal of trouble to pull her out, for she was out of her depth, and I made several snatches at her without effect. With the first good hold, however, I succeeded, but not before her breath was almost gone; and I supported her on my knee, to allow the water to run out of her mouth. At this moment, her little daughter, (half as old as herself, so much for early marriages,) who had just heard of the accident, came flying across the vessels, and seizing her mother by the shoulders, " Mother, mother," said she, " how came you to fall in ?" The poor woman's speech had not returned, and the more she gasped for breath, the more the little girl persevered in shaking her, repeating her question with a froward animation and eagerness, expressive of the truest affection and anxiety. In a few minutes, the woman was quite well, and lamenting her wet clothes.

About twelve o'clock at night, some of the company at the ball began to move off, each damsel chaperoned by her partner. Some, perhaps because they were more fatigued, or having farther to go, lay down in pairs on the floor at the end of the room, to rest themselves till morning. Before one o'clock, not less than a dozen of the dancers were in this manner recumbent,—and it was all considered proper. " What Mrs. Grundy would say " to it is another matter.

July 5th to 6th.—It was unfortunate that the gentlemen whose business it was to load the schooner, had been among the principal beaux at the ball the night before, and it was more unlucky, that they required an entire day to recover from their fatigue. The schooner lay at the wharf the whole of the morning of the 5th, quite deserted, without even a boy in a red night-cap to answer interrogatories. The festival of Independence comes only once a-year, and the people of all sorts seem to make the most of it. However, early on the morning of the 6th, barrels were seen trundling merrily towards the water's edge; and before three in the afternoon, we sailed with a favourable breeze out of the harbour. Before sunset we were quite out of sight of land, and to all appearance as much at sea as if we had been in the middle of the Atlantic. The master of the vessel, as the night came on, determined to lay-to until the morning. Had we made the islands called the False Ducks before dark, we should have stood on for Kingston Harbour.

July 7th.—At daylight we proceeded on our voyage, and anchored, at nine o'clock in the morning, at Kingston. I heard that Colonel P—— was just about to leave Kingston, in a batteau, for Montreal, and it was proposed to me to accompany him; an arrangement which suited me in every way. So, having breakfasted on shore, we were all in the batteau and ready to depart before eleven o'clock. Our batteau was a large flat-bottomed boat, pointed at both ends alike, and manned entirely by French Canadians. The wind was favourable, and we had a large sail to assist us; so that we very soon had an opportunity of hearing a genuine Canadian boat-song. In it there was a vast deal more noise than music, nor of all others that I heard these men sing during the voyage, did the melodies bear the slightest resemblance to any I had heard before. The *refrein* of one of these songs I happen to recollect, and it is as follows:

Sommes nous au   mi - lieu   du   bois,

Sommes nous au   ri - vage - - e.

This they roared out without mercy, in full chorus, and one at a time sang the song itself, which treated of the hardihood of the Voyageurs, the troubles and difficulties they encounter, not forgetting their skill and bravery in surmounting them. We had a pleasant voyage down this noble river, where the " Thousand islands " present a prospect of land and water, as if a recent deluge had inundated the country. We went about thirty miles, when we put up for the night at an inn adjoining the shore.

July 8th.—We proceeded down the river as far as Prescott.

July 9th.—The rapidity of the stream had now so considerably increased, that we might well have expected to encounter the Rapids, towards which we were quickly advancing. At last the roar of the Rapide Plât was distinctly heard; a heavy sullen sound like that of the sea; and the surface of the water, though gliding onwards with extreme velocity, was level and smooth in the current, but at the same time full of little eddies and whirlpools. And so we glanced along till we pitched down at once into the Rapid. *" A terre,"* *" A large,"* was now the cry, as the steersman gave his directions to the men to

keep the head of the batteau on or off the
land; and every man tugged hard, and worked with great animation till we were through
the rough water and again in tranquillity.
We afterwards passed the Longue Saut,
through a channel so full of rocks and shoals
that no vessel but a flat-bottomed boat could
possibly have lived in it. Sometimes we
seemed on the point of being dashed against
the land, till, snatched away by some unseen
eddy into another direction, we were twisted
down a watery precipice, and carried across
a bubbling field of waves and breakers, till
once more in open space the lessening roar of
waters died upon the ear, and the beauties of
the surrounding scenery again burst upon the
sight.

As our batteau was shooting along at a
most rapid rate, we came suddenly upon a
point of land where three deer had stepped
down to the water's edge to drink. The timid
creatures stood quite still and looked at us as
we passed within a very few yards of them,—of
so little importance, amid the noise and crash

of water, was a boat with near a dozen men in it!

Although none of the considerable Rapids can be passed without a severe struggle for a boat, (unless one of large size,) there is no real danger, and accidents are seldom heard of. It is an undertaking which most men would encounter once for the sake of curiosity, but very few would repeat for pleasure. The scale of things is infinitely large, and the expanse of water so great, that cascades, whirlpools, and bubbling gulfs, are changing places with each other in the uncontrollable variety of an obstructed torrent. Although the main stream remains always the same, the effect produced by the back currents and eddies is so different, that boat after boat submits as it were to the caprice of fate, and, like feathers in the air, no two together can ever possibly follow the same identical course. —We proceeded this day as far as Cornwall, where we put up for the night.

July 10th. — We had passed Lake St.

Francis, the Côteau du Lac, and the Cedar
Rapids, and we were carried along not only
by the rapidity of the stream, but by the assistance of our sail. The wind had been
against us, but had now become favourable;
at the same time the clouds seemed to threaten
us with a thunder storm. As we had not
many miles to proceed to the town of Cèdres,
the men pulled hard, and we made all the
way possible ; at the same time the sky grew
blacker, till it almost touched the water, and
the wind too increased very considerably. The
tempest was hanging on our rear as we flew
before it, and we arrived at Cèdres just in
time to run into the inn before the first big
drops, which were to be plainly seen falling a
few hundred yards behind us, had overtaken
our batteau. It was a severe storm, and
lasted a good while. In the meantime we
dined, and in about a couple of hours, the
weather having quite cleared up, although
the evening was advancing, we re-embarked,
intending to pass the night at La Chine. The

men took some time to arrange themselves in their places ; but in a little while all seemed right, and we were drifting with great velocity towards the verge of the Cascades' Rapid ; and, when it was too late to stop, we found that half the men were quite drunk, and the steersman the worst of all the party ; so we were obliged to snatch the oars from these men and do as well as we could for ourselves ; and I never saw a more cowardly set of rascals than the boatmen. They absolutely cried till they roared, and were as helpless as a parcel of children. In the mean time we had got into the middle of the torrent, which was sufficiently ill-treating us ; but, by pulling hard and holding water, we kept the boat's head right so as to get through the Rapid at the expense of a good wetting. But we had wandered altogether out of our course, and had fairly lost our way upon the river, which became extremely wide, and divided by the intervening land into several channels : and thus we pulled on at a venture till it grew

quite dark. We were then on the opposite
bank of the river, and gave up all hopes of
crossing over back again to La Chine. At
last we came to the mouth of the Châteaugay
River, which we entered, and found out a
miserable house, where we passed the night
in our clothes, among swarms of mosquitoes,
dirt, and all sorts of untidiness.

July 11th.—We were glad enough to leave
this place, and had crossed the St. Lawrence
and landed at La Chine before six o'clock in
the morning. Here I got a comfortable
breakfast, and, finding I was within nine miles
of Montreal, I hired a calash to take me thither. It was a high, clumsy-looking buggy,
with head, apron, &c., and built apparently
with little regard to weight. The wheels
were excessively high, and there was a small
seat in front for the driver, who rested his
legs on the shafts across the horse's rump. A
stout grey cob took us along at a very good
pace, and I arrived at Montreal in time to
take my place in the steam-boat, which was

to move at two o'clock the next morning for Quebec,—the passengers to be all on board at eight o'clock. I dined at a table d'hôte, and went on board.

July 12th to 13th.—We arrived so late at night at Quebec, that none of the passengers went on shore on the 12th; but on the morning of the 13th I landed under a very different temperature than prevailed on the day when I had last crossed the river among the ice, in the log-canoe. On that day, in the winter, the thermometer stood at least twelve or fifteen degrees below zero of Fahrenheit; it was now at ninety-five in the shade.

Having got a passage for England on board a transport ship of 200 tons, (the crew consisting of six men and a boy,) we weighed anchor on the 29th, and, after tacking about for twenty-four hours in a fog off the mouth of the river, (among a parcel of other ships, all of us ringing bells and beating drums,) and weathering a stiff gale on the Banks of Newfoundland, we made a good passage, and reached soundings on the 27th August. At daybreak on the 28th we made the island of Guernsey, which the master had mistaken for the Lizard. Laying to for the night off Portland light-house, we set sail the next morning, the 29th, and I landed safely at Portsmouth about noon.

CONCLUDING REMARKS ON EMIGRATION.

To have lived in North America without forming a favourable estimate of the advantages possessed by the poor of that country over those of our own, is quite impossible; nor can it be wondered at, that the condition of the labouring classes should be better in a land where the inhabitants bear so different a proportion to the cultivated soil. At the present day, while Nature points out to the dense population of Europe an expanse where her surplus numbers might spread themselves abroad to any degree of extent, the art of man seems to second her efforts, by divesting locomotion of its difficulties; so that an abstract question urges itself more and more every day on the mind, on contemplating the face of the universal globe, why the human race should continue to be distributed with such extreme inequality upon its surface.

Without presuming to determine on the general expediency of a system of emigration, it may not be amiss to urge one or two brief remarks, founded on local observation, on some of the objections which at first sight appear to be arrayed against it : and first, as regards the severity of climate. This does, in fact, make age, state of family, constitution, &c., very important considerations to persons intending to undertake the life of a settler; although, as applied to practical reasoning, it has been in all probability extremely over-rated and exaggerated. To a traveller, the difference of temperature, under all the disadvantages to which he is subjected on his route, such as the being obliged to inhabit houses hastily raised, huts, &c., and being constantly, from his unsettled habits, ill protected in every way from the weather; these circumstances, I say, form no fair criterion as to the effect of the temperature on the constitution; and it is quite as unreasonable to institute a comparison between him and the settler, as to compare the life of a soldier in the field with that of a citizen in a populous town.

Every climate is unhealthy where men are insufficiently protected from the weather; on the contrary, the being well housed and provided with fuel is more than an equivalent for extreme severity of cold. To some of the hardiest animals Nature assigns the warmest habitations. As to the human race, in appreciating the value of warmth, we need not go farther than take the peasantry of England and Ireland. Why are the poor of the latter country confessedly more robust, although more ill fed, than the former? Doubtless because the walls of the mud cabin are impervious to the weather, while its inmates are provided with sufficient fuel. The cottage of the English pauper is usually a straggling, ill-contrived building; his fuel is scanty, and the consequence is, that rheumatism reigns the endemic disease of the country. Taking, therefore, into consideration the quantity of timber for firewood at the disposal of the settler in the North American colonies, it will appear, on critical examination, that the climate is a healthy one, and that no experience, founded on well-conducted experiment, has hitherto proved to the contrary.

But if, on the one hand, too rigid objections have been urged against the climate, there is another point towards which perhaps too little attention has been directed; namely, the very opposite interests existing between the emigrant and the colonial land-owner; and this, notwithstanding that it is of great importance as to any general system of emigration, if such were ever to be either actively promoted or indirectly encouraged. It certainly does appear, as a general principle, unquestionable, that the emigrant should not be in any way subjected to men who have objects of their own in locating the country at variance with his interest. In a country where land exists to such an unlimited extent, its value must, of course, almost entirely depend upon its cultivated or uncultivated state, also upon its proximity to the already settled parts of the country; so that an emigrant cannot possibly enrich himself by clearing his own land, without at the same time adding a value to his neighbour's property, and that in a proportion of which here we can form little idea. Upon this principle it is that motives of personal interest have, to say the least of them, an indirect influence upon the locating of emigrants in the country. Men are encouraged to leave their own homes, unfitted by age and constitution to endure the change of habits and climate; and, for want of sound disinterested advice when they arrive in the country, meet with difficulty after difficulty, till they become embarrassed and in debt, and finally fall victims to misery and misdirected speculation.

To a healthy, but severe climate, none but the young should venture,—children, and men and women under five-and-twenty. In after age, the change of climate is in itself a trial to the health; and as Nature decrees in vegetative life, so man himself must be transplanted early, or the experiment will not thrive. Nevertheless, supposing the case of an infirm person making the adventure, it is not impossible but that he may advance the interests of the colonial land-owner, in whatever degree he may mar his own : the former may find a way to turn his labour to advantage, for sure enough it is, that so long as one man can be found to sow, another will appear in due course to reap.

Within the enormous stretch of the British North American colonies, spots eligible in all respects for the purposes of the emigrant may be said everywhere to abound. He requires a good agricultural position, not too far removed from the cultivated lands. The growth of the pine points out the poor land, while that of the birch, maple, and the harder woods, is a sufficient indication of the richer soil. But his first object, surely, is to reach the place of his future domicile, at as little expense as possible both of time and money. Yet, if the colonial land-owner yields to motives of self-interest, he will naturally be led to determine upon a position for the emigrant, be it ever so remote, so long as it is best calculated to advance his own interest or that of the particular part of the country he happens to live in ; and to this cause, which does, in fact, prevail in some degree all over the country, the Fur companies contribute their share also, many persons, in different ways interested in their operations, having an additional object in locating settlers in distant points along the present thread of settlement, for the protection of their voyageurs and the encouragement of their trade.

While men emigrate in dribblets, unsupported by disinterested advice, and without the means of establishing themselves independently at once on their arrival, there are many ways by which any speculative land-jobber may enrich himself at their expense. Let a case be supposed, for instance, where a man has ten thousand acres to locate, and he divides the whole " block " into a hundred lots, of a hundred acres each, out of which he disposes of eighty lots, reserving to himself twenty lots, or two thousand acres. Now, he takes care that these two thousand acres shall be so intermingled and entangled with the rest as to present little desirable patches, which every tenant, as he rises in the world, would be desirous to purchase, and they are accordingly doled out as they are required at an exorbitant rate ; and thus a heavy profit is exacted out of the hard labour of the emigrant, not only to the great detriment of the individual, but the discouragement of emigration in general. Such partial instances tend directly to bring any thing like system into disrepute, which never can have its full force till means are devised to secure to the settlers themselves that increase in the value of land which arises out of the act of location, and in the present state of things very generally finds its way into the pockets of the colonial land-owners.

Against this description of persons collectively these trifling and general remarks are by no means intended to convey to the public an unfavourable opinion, being a set of men, I verily believe, as honourable in their dealings as others in any part of the known world ; but we are not to expect too much of human

nature. " Ships are but boards, pilots men ;"
and people will not neglect their own interests,
forget their lands, their roads, and their
bridges, called upon so often as they must be
to become judges in their own cause, and determine whether the settler shall mend the
land, or whether the land shall mend the settler. Were a system of emigration once to
be set on foot, which could confine and secure
to the parties concerned the enormous increase
in value of the land in the surrounding neighbourhood of the locations, it might very probably ere long go alone and help itself ; and
I am not sure but that, upon the principle of
extending our parochial establishments to
North America, as far as regards the young
and able dependant upon public bounty, something like a modification of our poor-laws, ap-
plicable both to England and Ireland, might
be contrived. In the mean time, whatever
future policy on the subject may direct, there
must be always prejudices to be encountered
peculiar to ourselves as islanders ; for, instead
of inuring ourselves by degrees to visit distant

points as our continental neighbours, the " cras ingens iterabimus æquor," appears, as it were, a constant placard, which, no matter whether the traps and spring-guns be real or imaginary, equally serves to protract the commencement of enterprise and limit the extent of many an individual's peregrination.

But voluntary emigration must be worthy of some consideration, if it were only as a means of disposing of any surplus population which the temporary pressure of circumstances may at any time create : it may be well to regard it as the safety-valve by which relief is to be obtained in extreme cases, and at the present moment particularly, as regards the existing state of Ireland, and before the ope- ration of the disfranchisement bill can have assumed a salutary and healing form. My own abstract opinion can be worth but little ; nevertheless, having had an opportunity very lately of visiting almost every county in Ire- land, the result of my reflection was, upon observing the state of the poor, that there were no people in the world better calculated for a life in the North American forests than the Irish peasantry; none who could have less cause to regret the change,—a change, from the too narrow limits of a scanty, insufficient farm, for the unbounded range of space; none whose buoyancy of spirits, hardihood, love of enterprise, and frugality more eminently qualified them for the undertaking.

Besides, the disposition of the people has indisputably evinced of late years a tendency to emigrate, even enough to have already acquired sufficient force to be regarded as a serious political evil. Irish labourers have been in the habit of flocking every summer to our shores, in search of work and better wages than they can earn in their own country. To look a little deeper into the consequences of this fact, is it at all unreasonable to come at once to an ultimate conclusion, and say that the spirit of enterprise once stimulated will continue to advance, till men, becoming by degrees habituated to leave their homes and reap the advantages of employing their labour in distant parts, find objections to foreign residence gradually diminish every year, and in the end come to consider the Atlantic no greater an obstacle than the Irish Channel was in the beginning ? Thus, if the emigration of the Irish to England be not a preparatory step to advancing upon the more distant range of the North American colonies, it is at least consolatory to reflect, that inasmuch as the necessary provision for such an annual expense, trifling as it may be, must be met by correspondent habits of economy, such habits being seldom retrogressive, it follows that such tendency to emigrate does in the mean time mainly contribute to increase the stock of industry and moral virtue in a country sadly in want of such an exciting cause.

THE END.

G. Woodfall, Printer, Angel Court, Skinner Street, London.